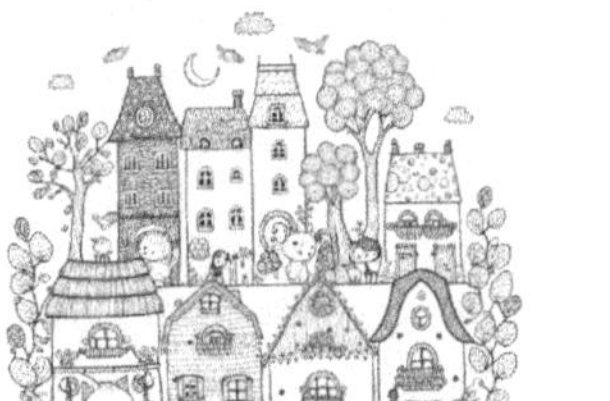
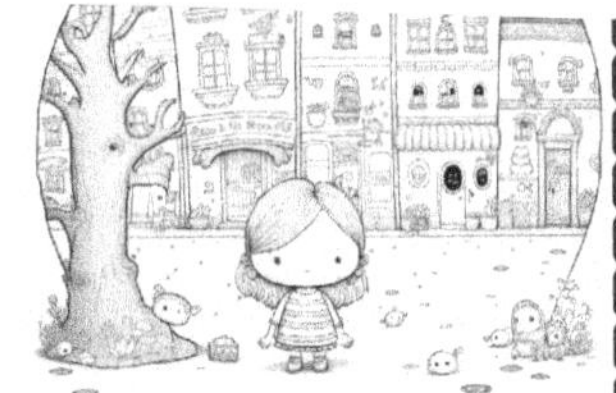

This Book Belongs To

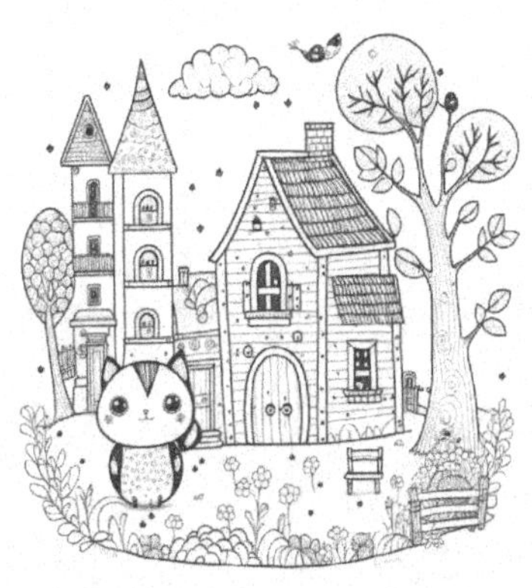
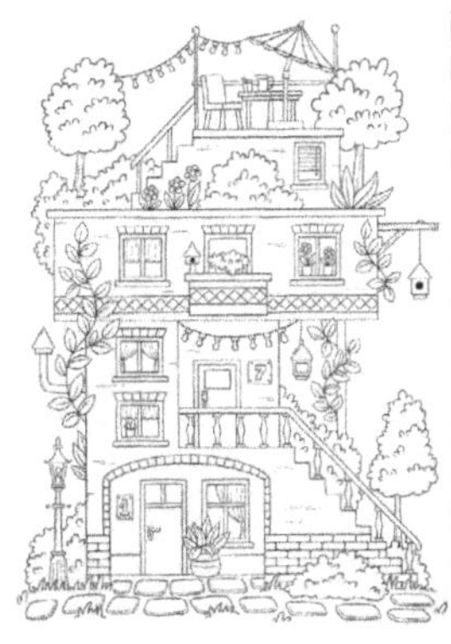

ADORABLE TOWN COLORING BOOK

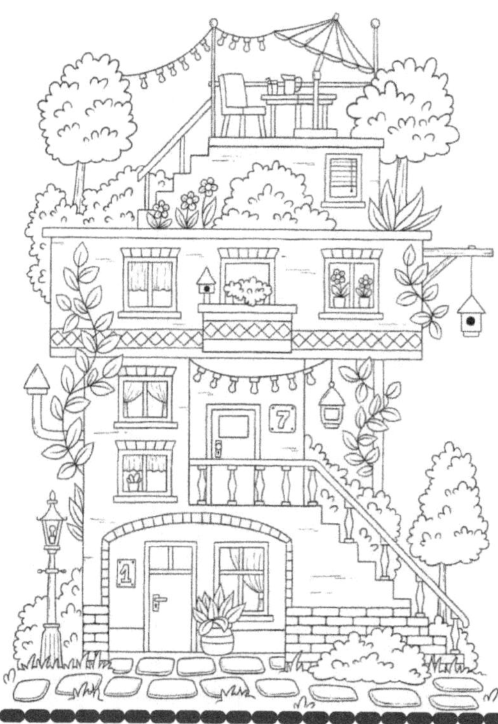

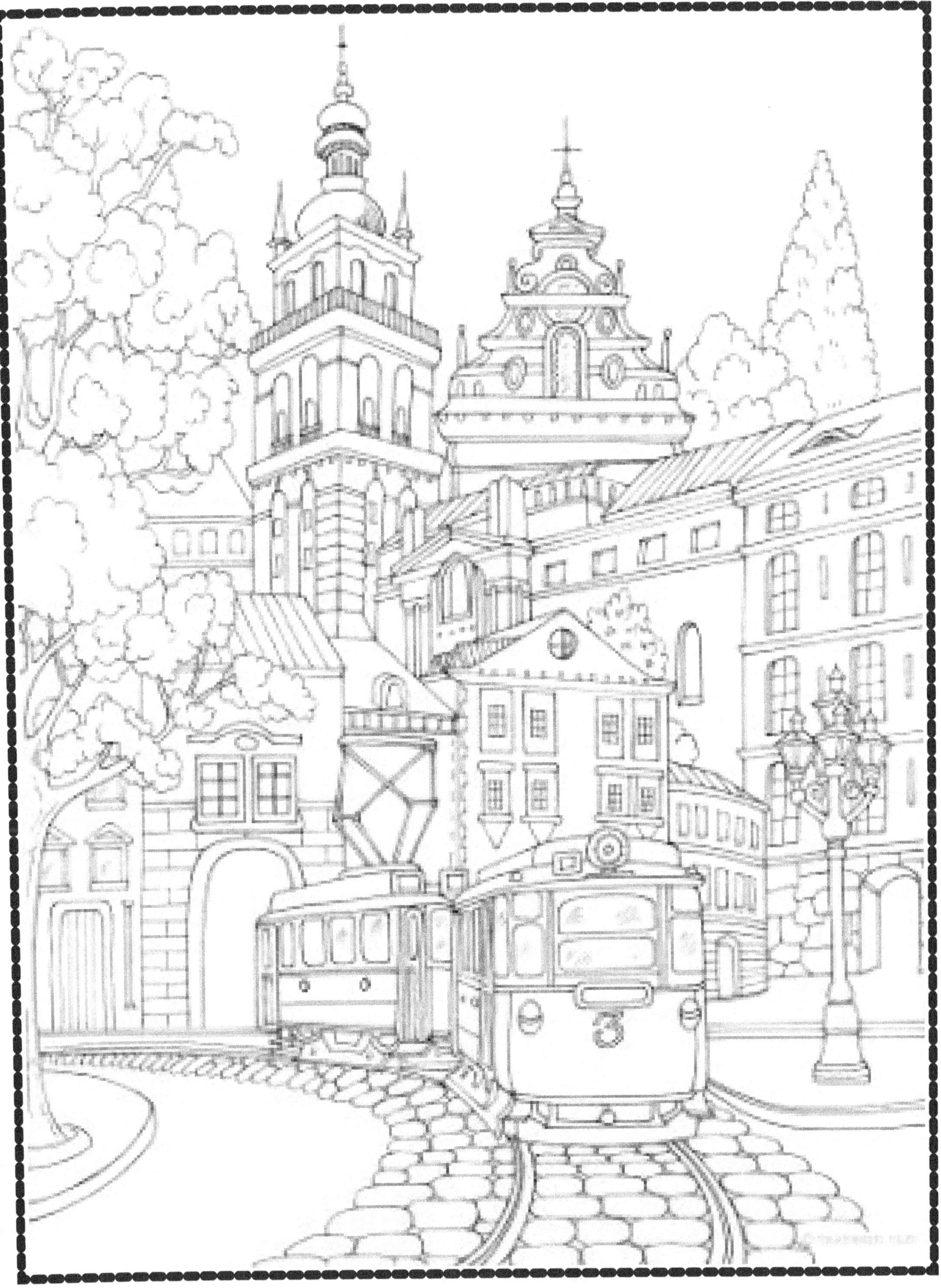

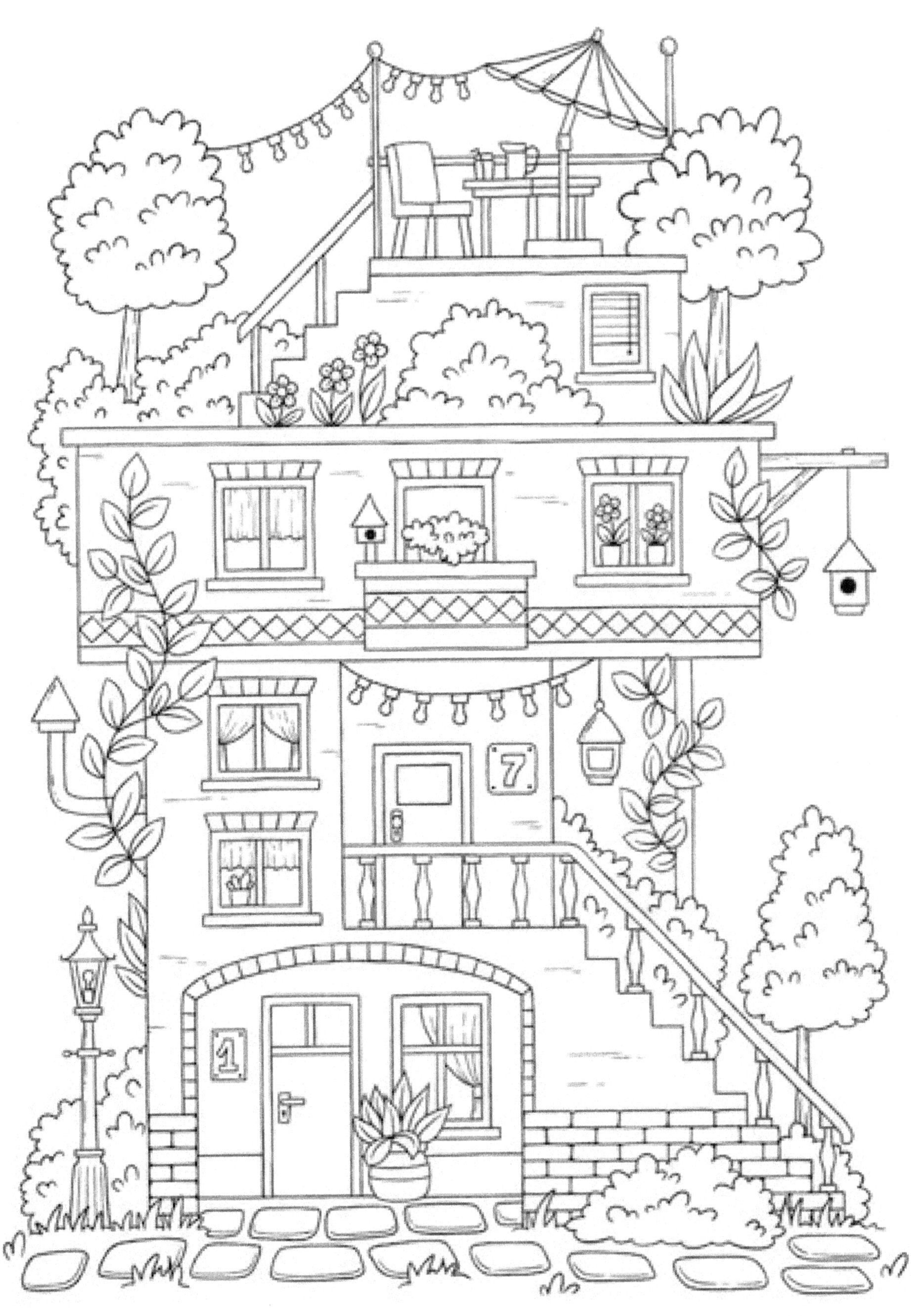

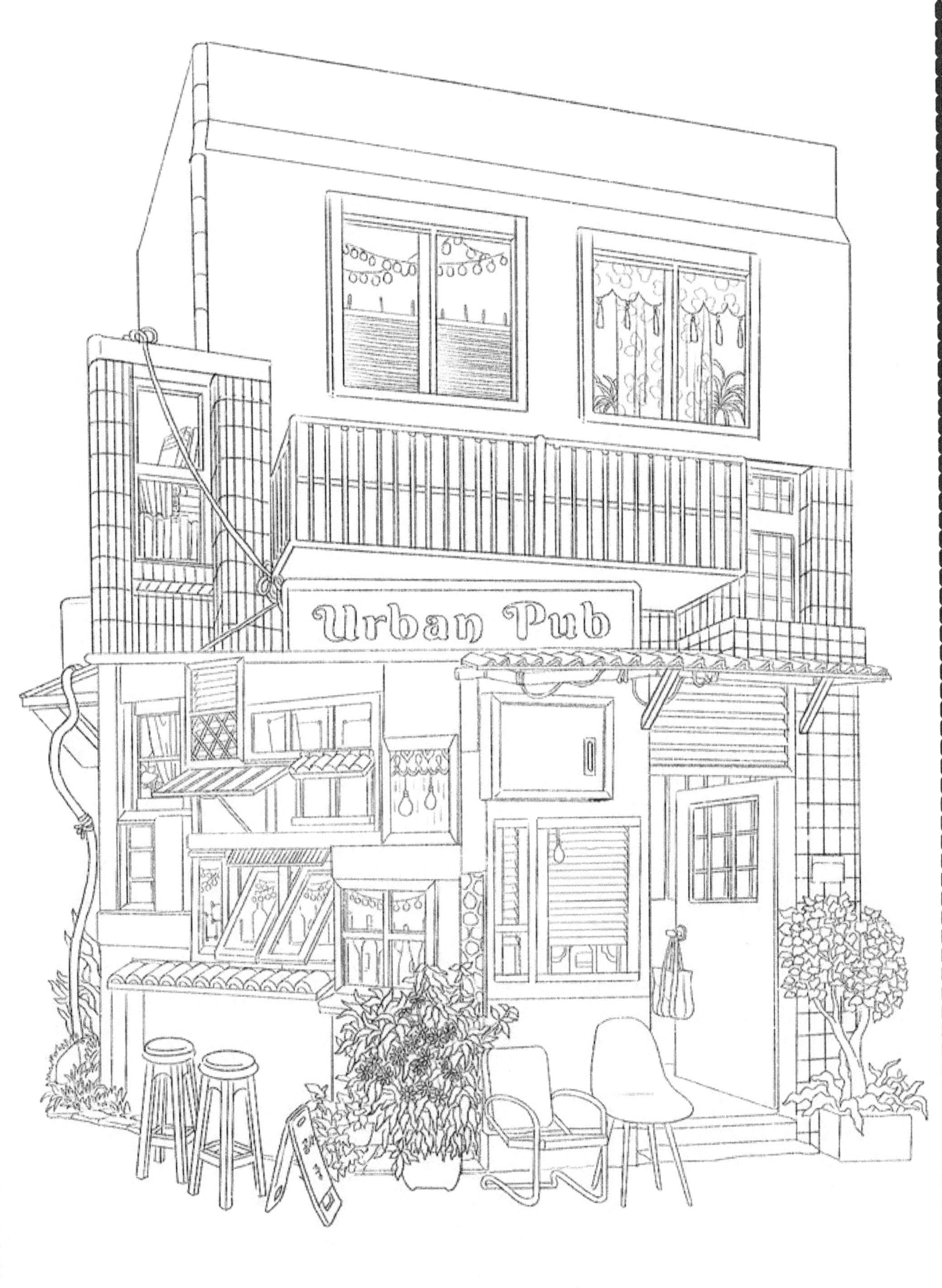
Urban Pub

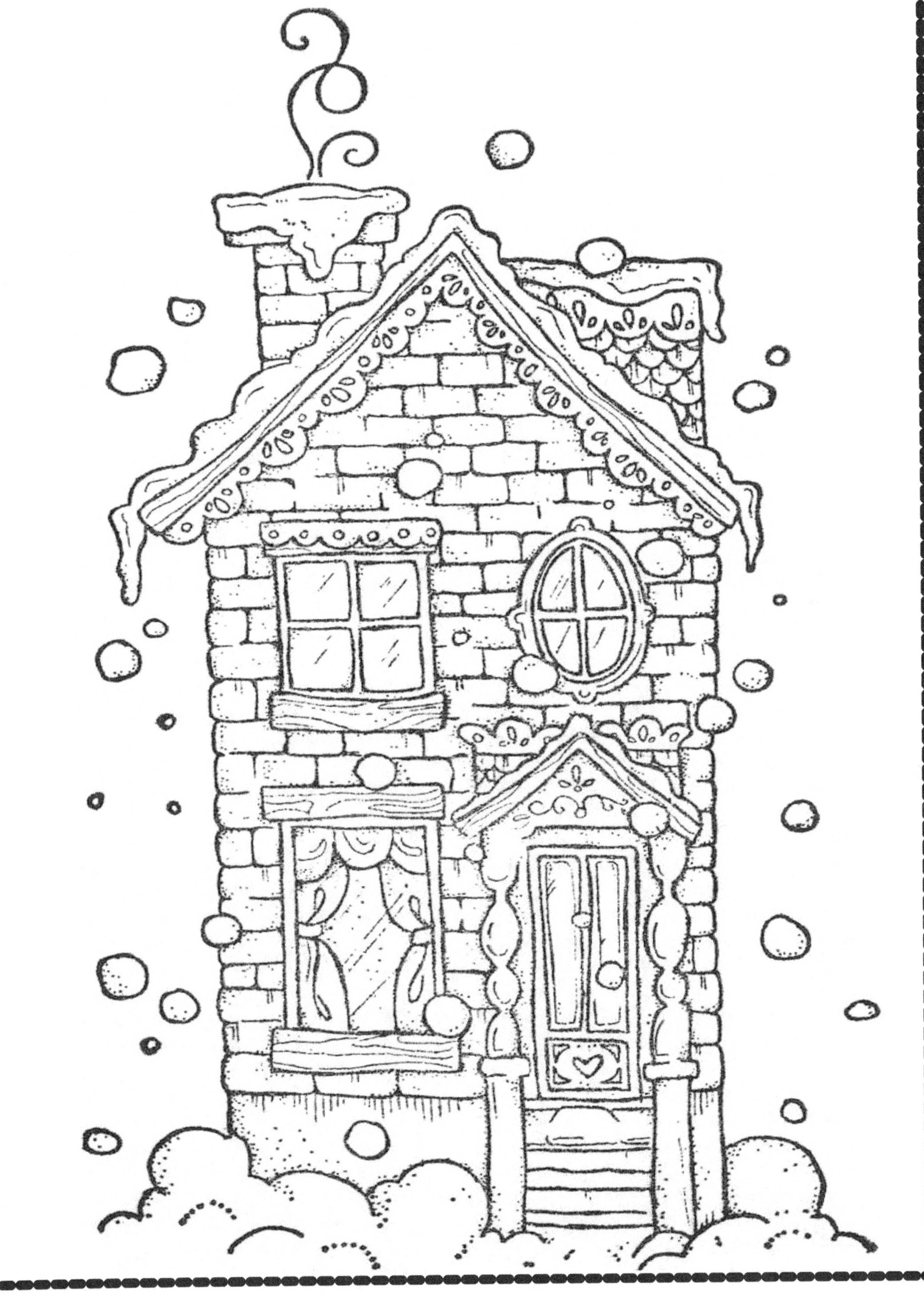

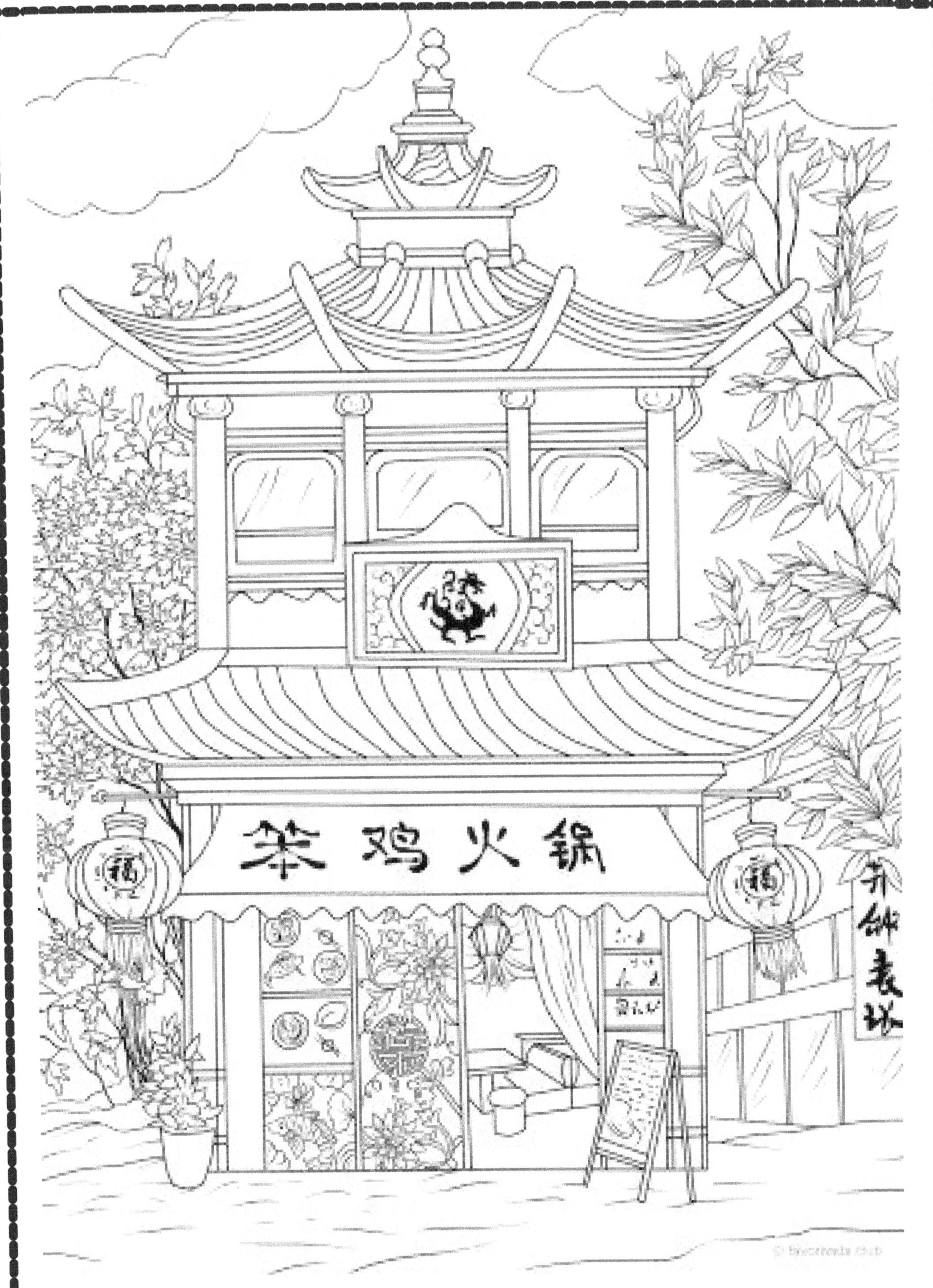

笨 鸡 火 锅
福
福

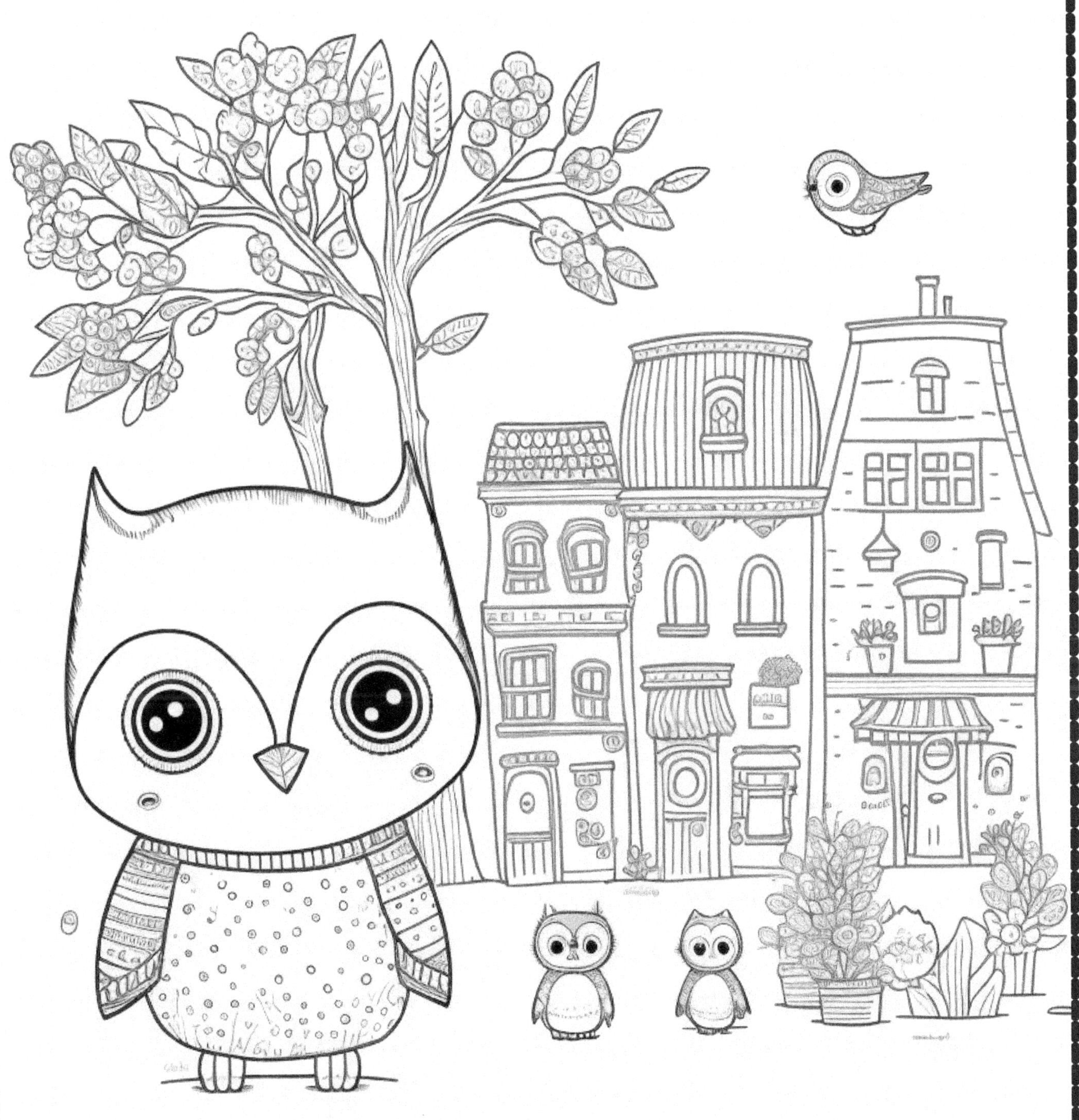

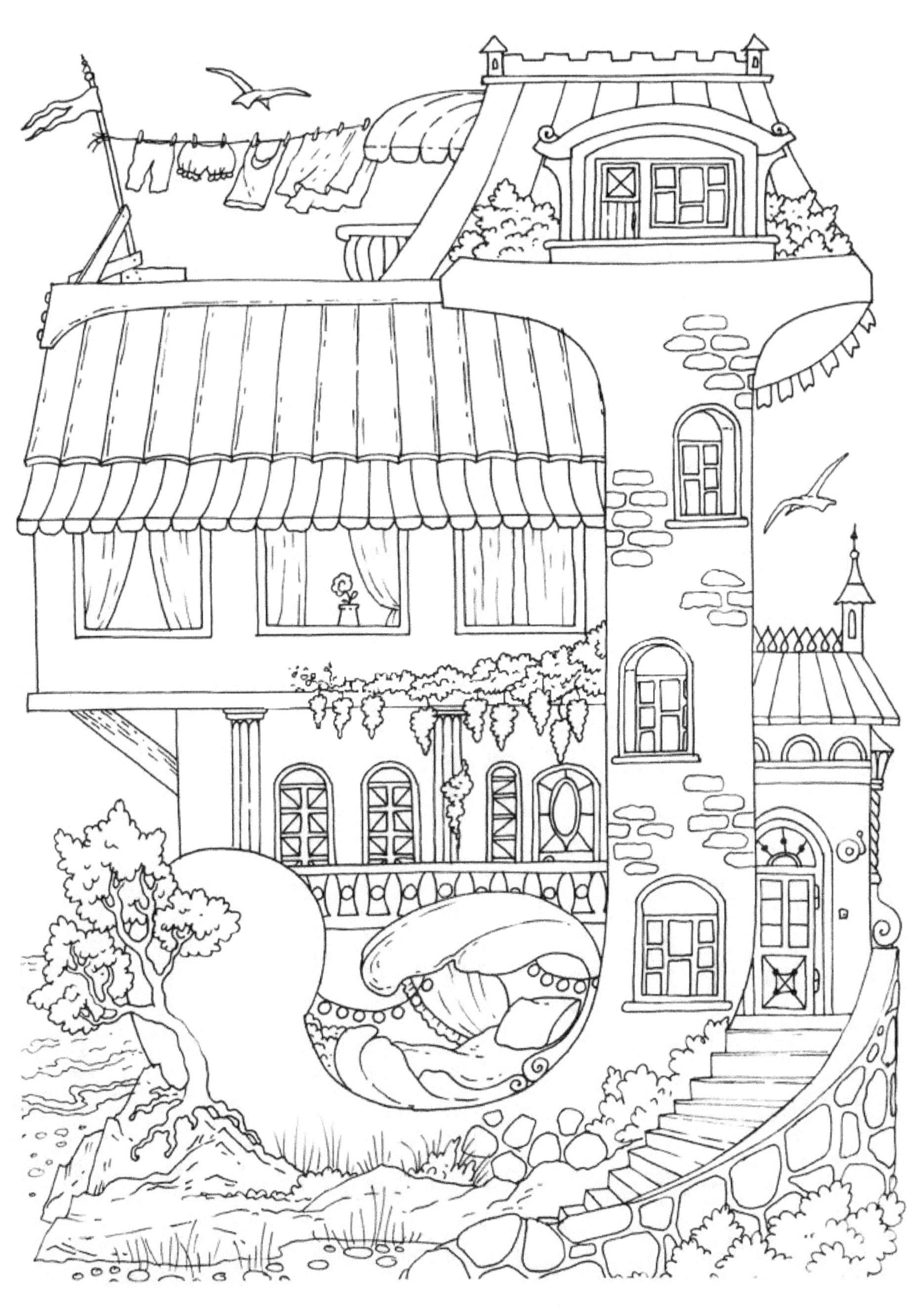

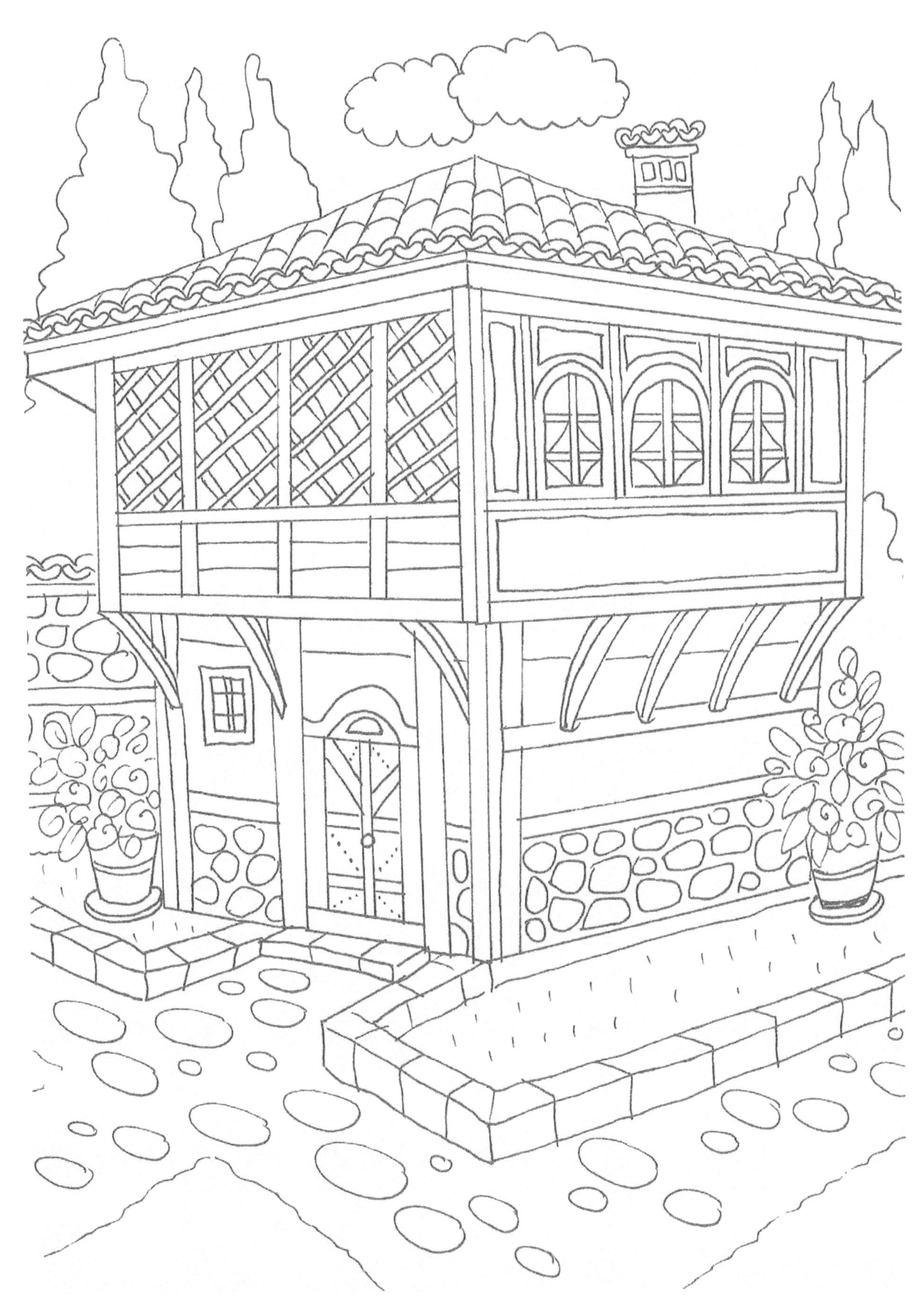

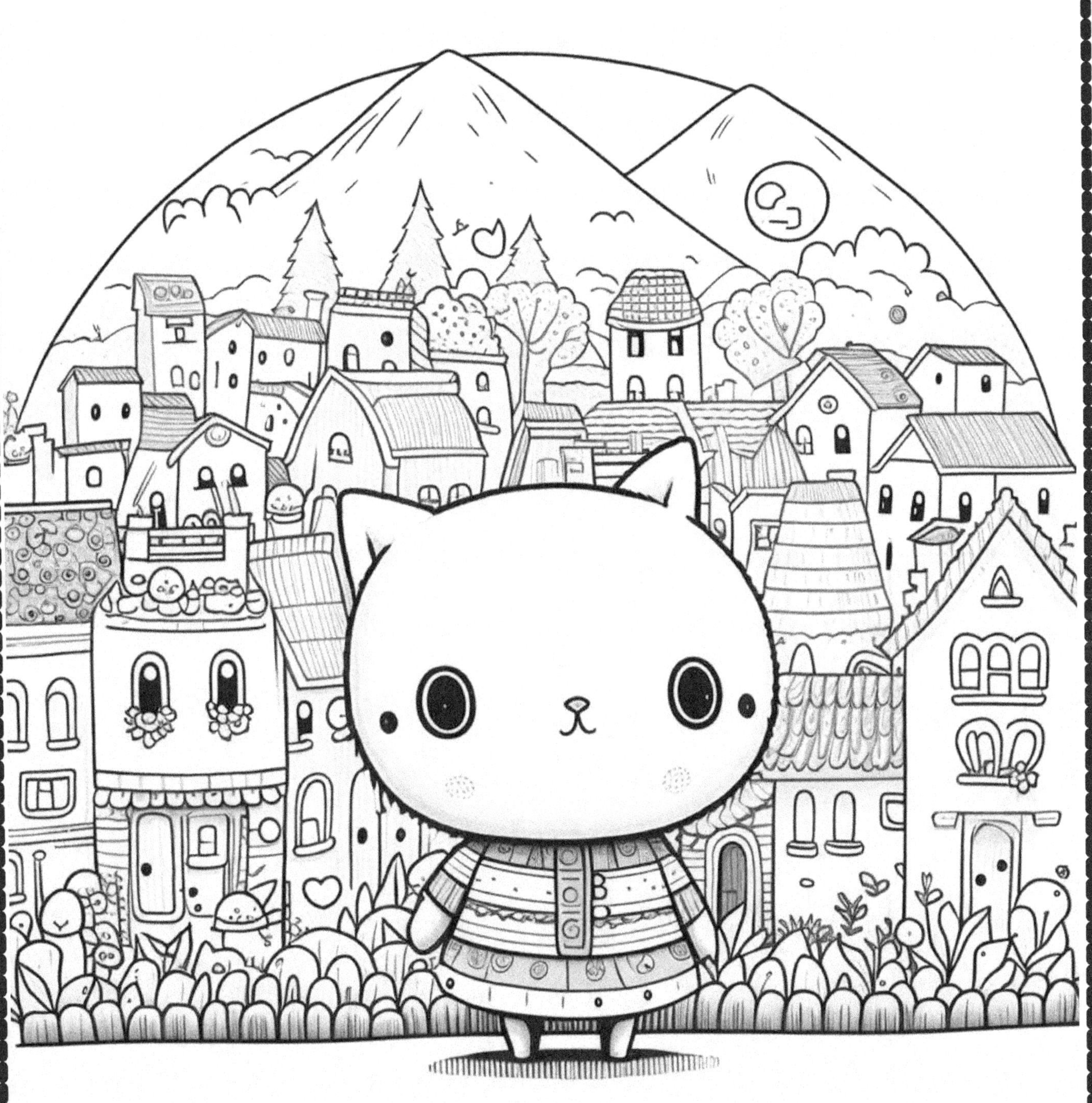

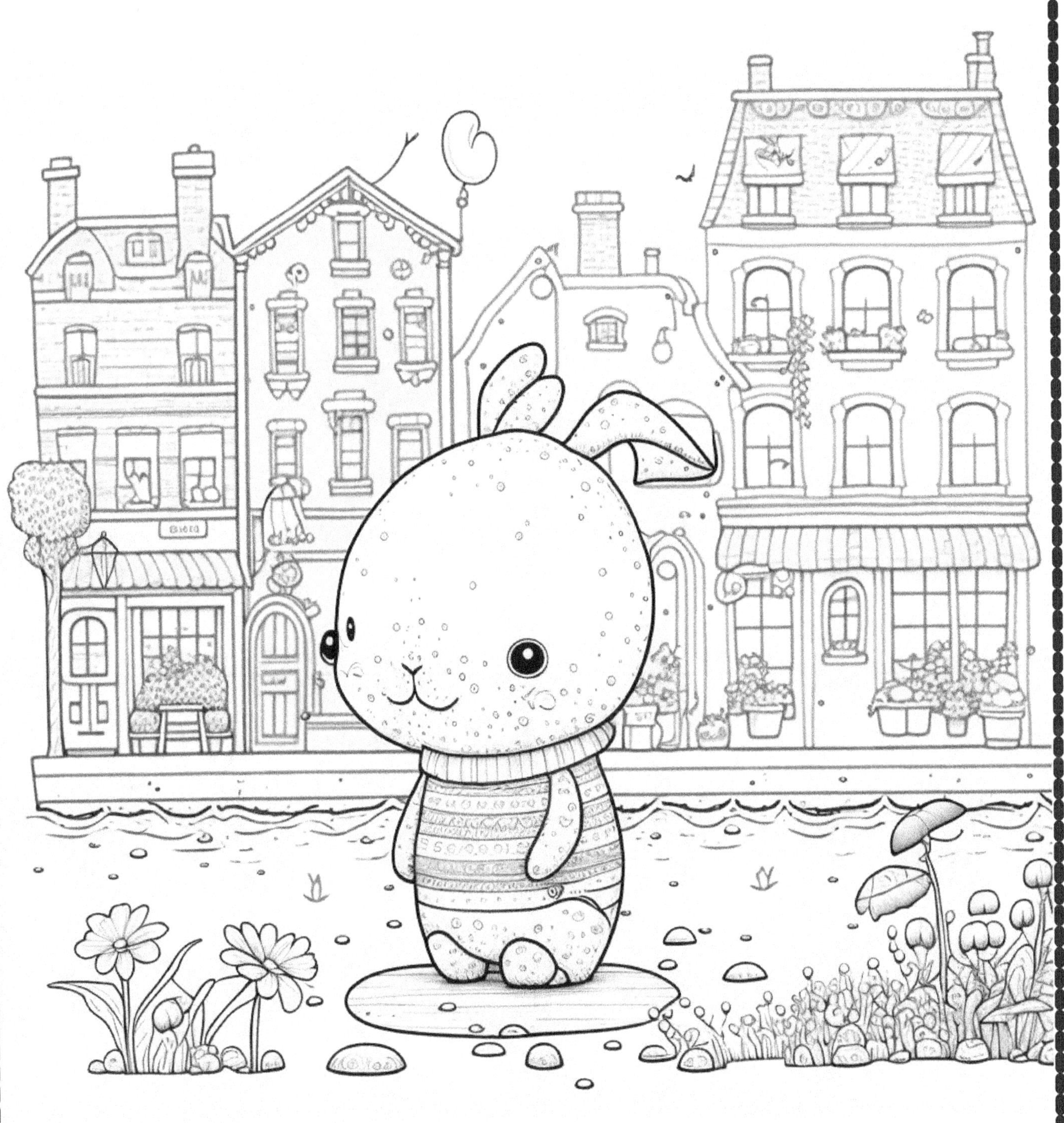

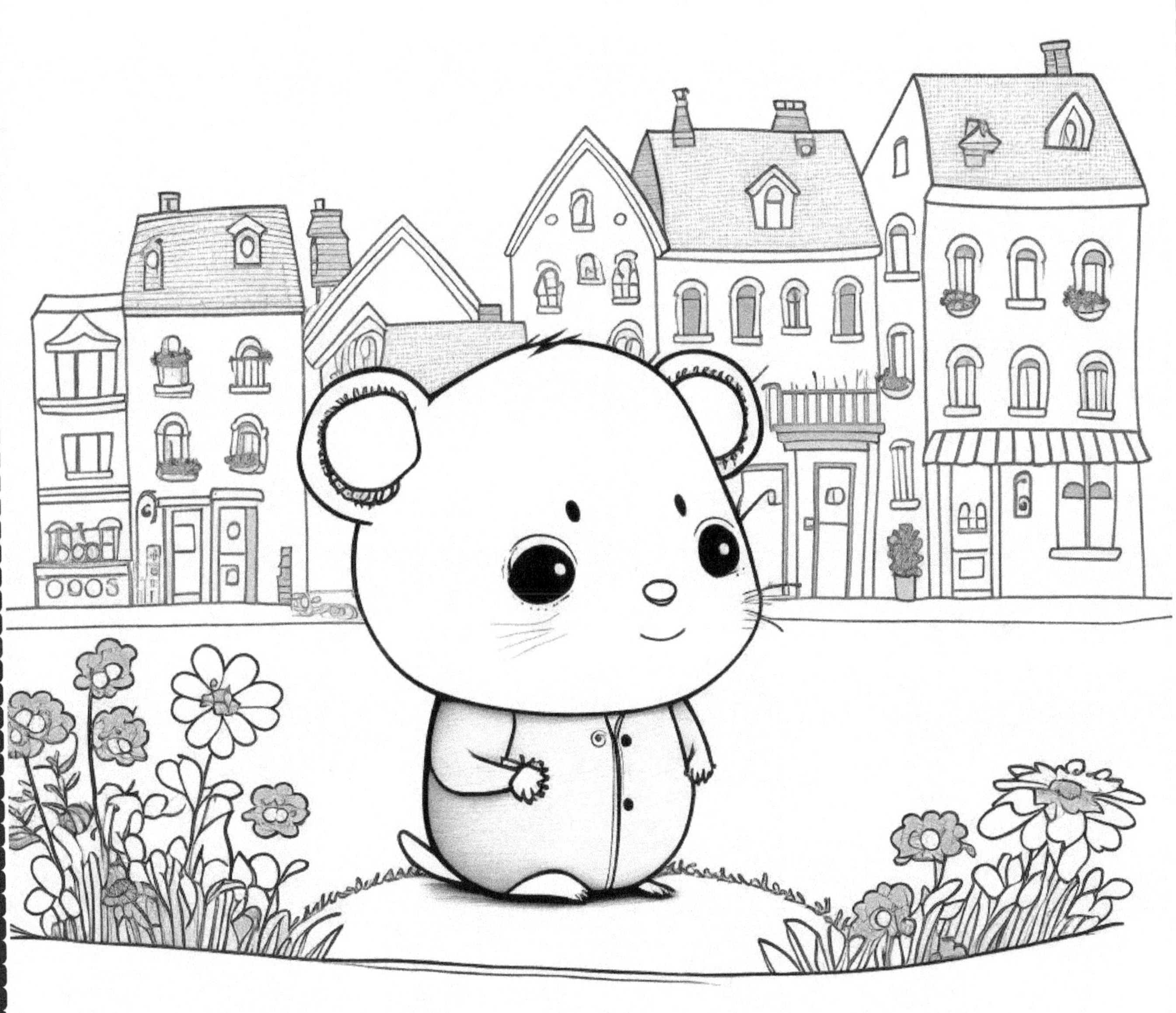

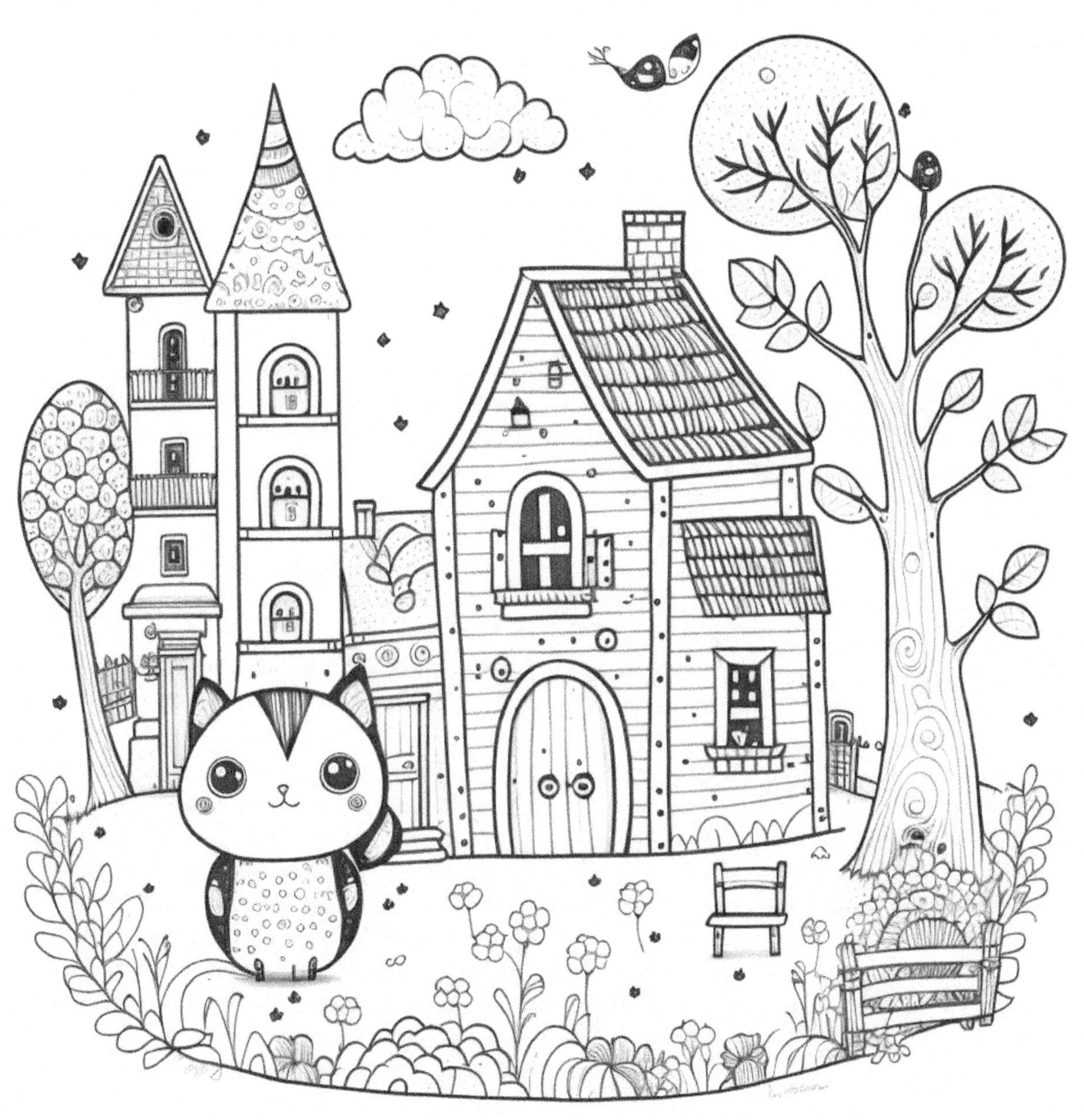

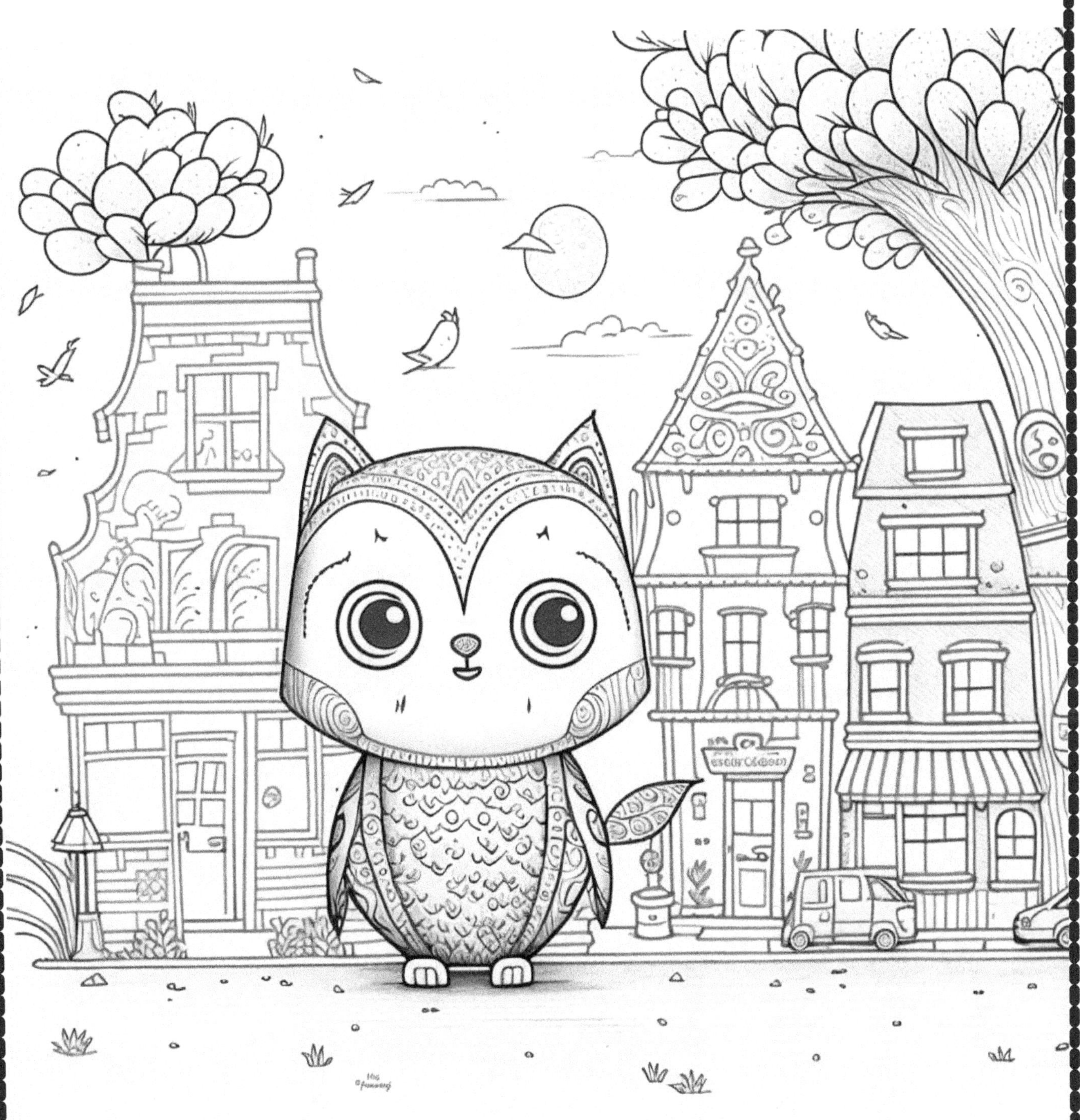

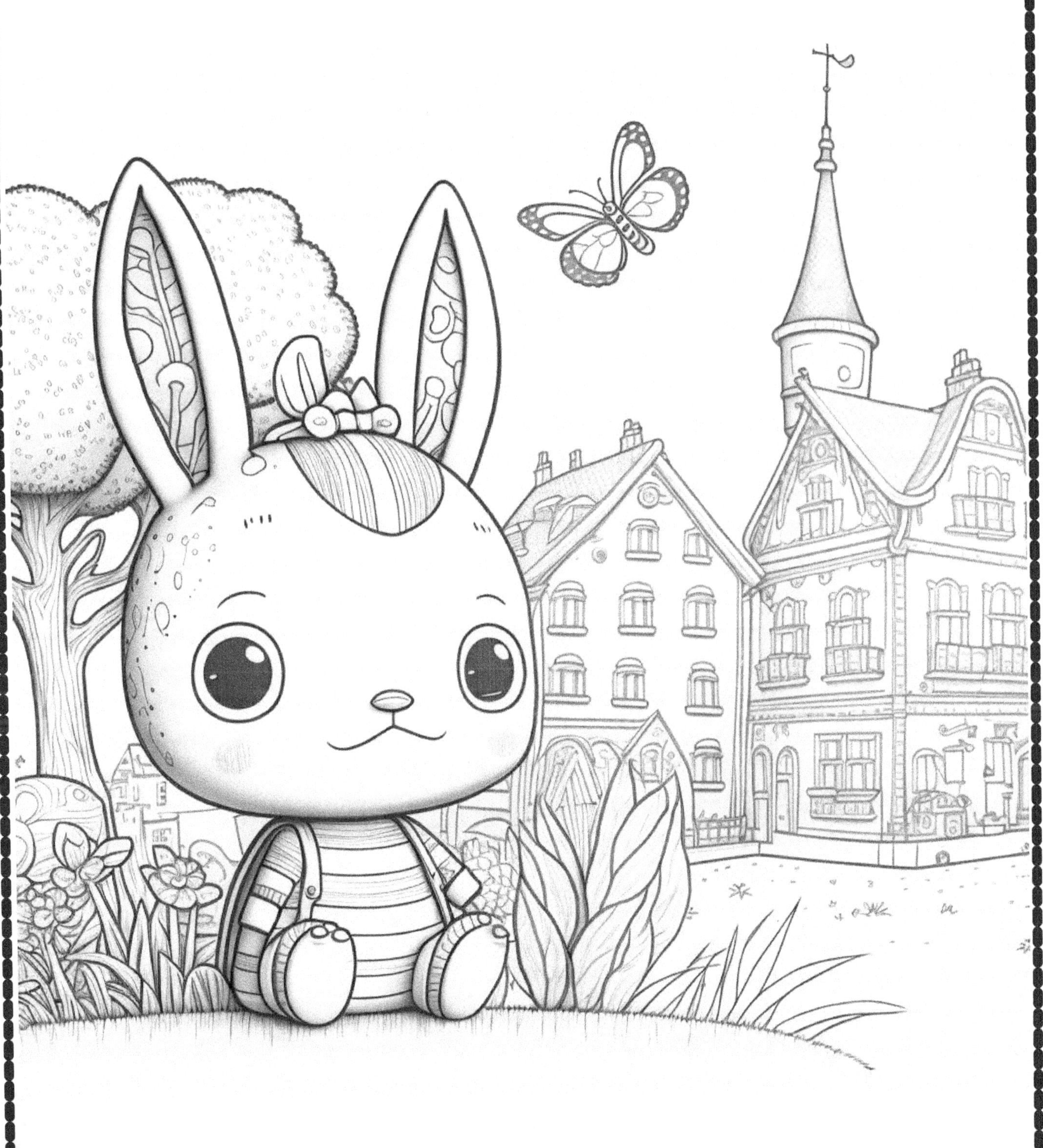

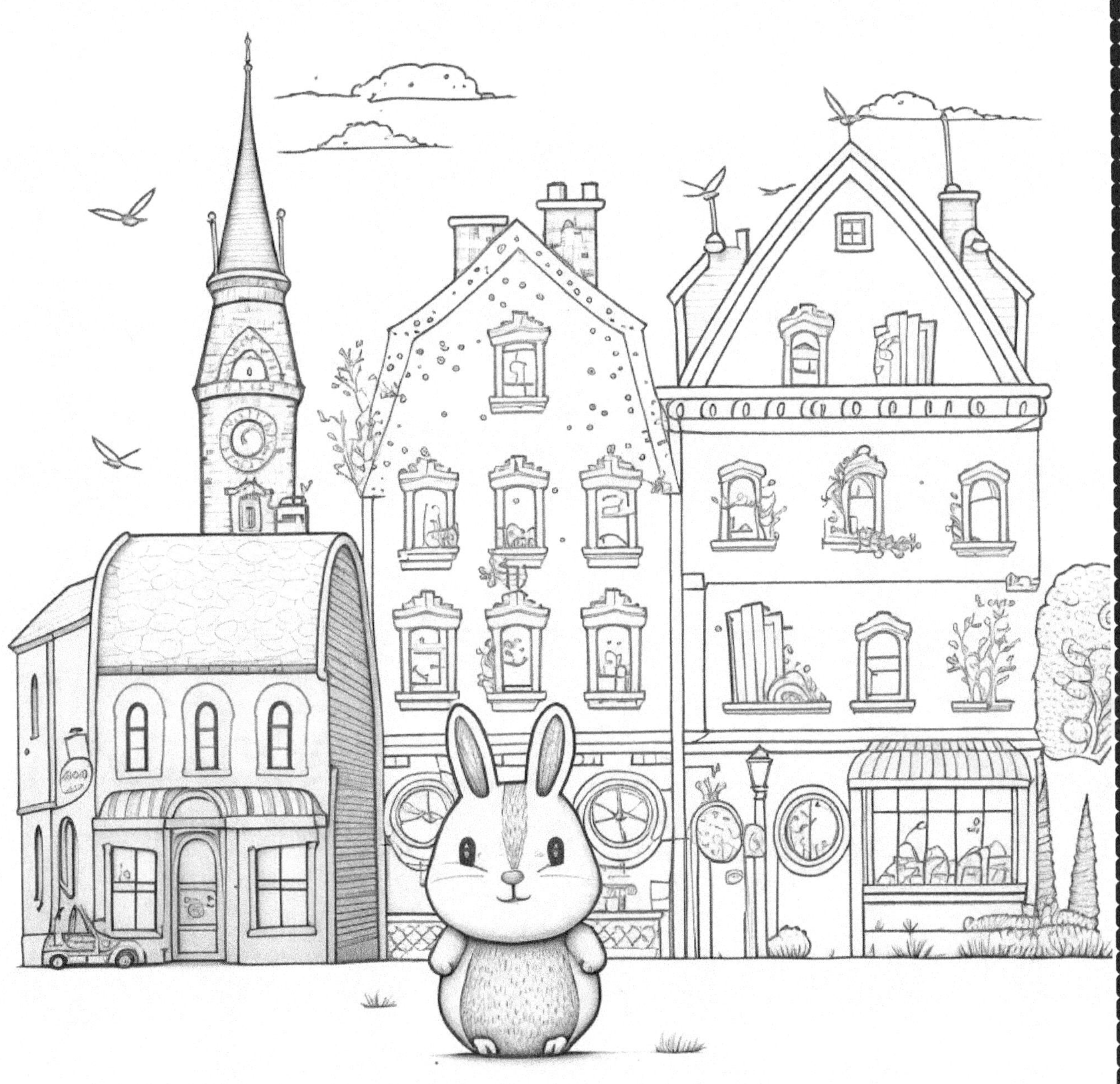

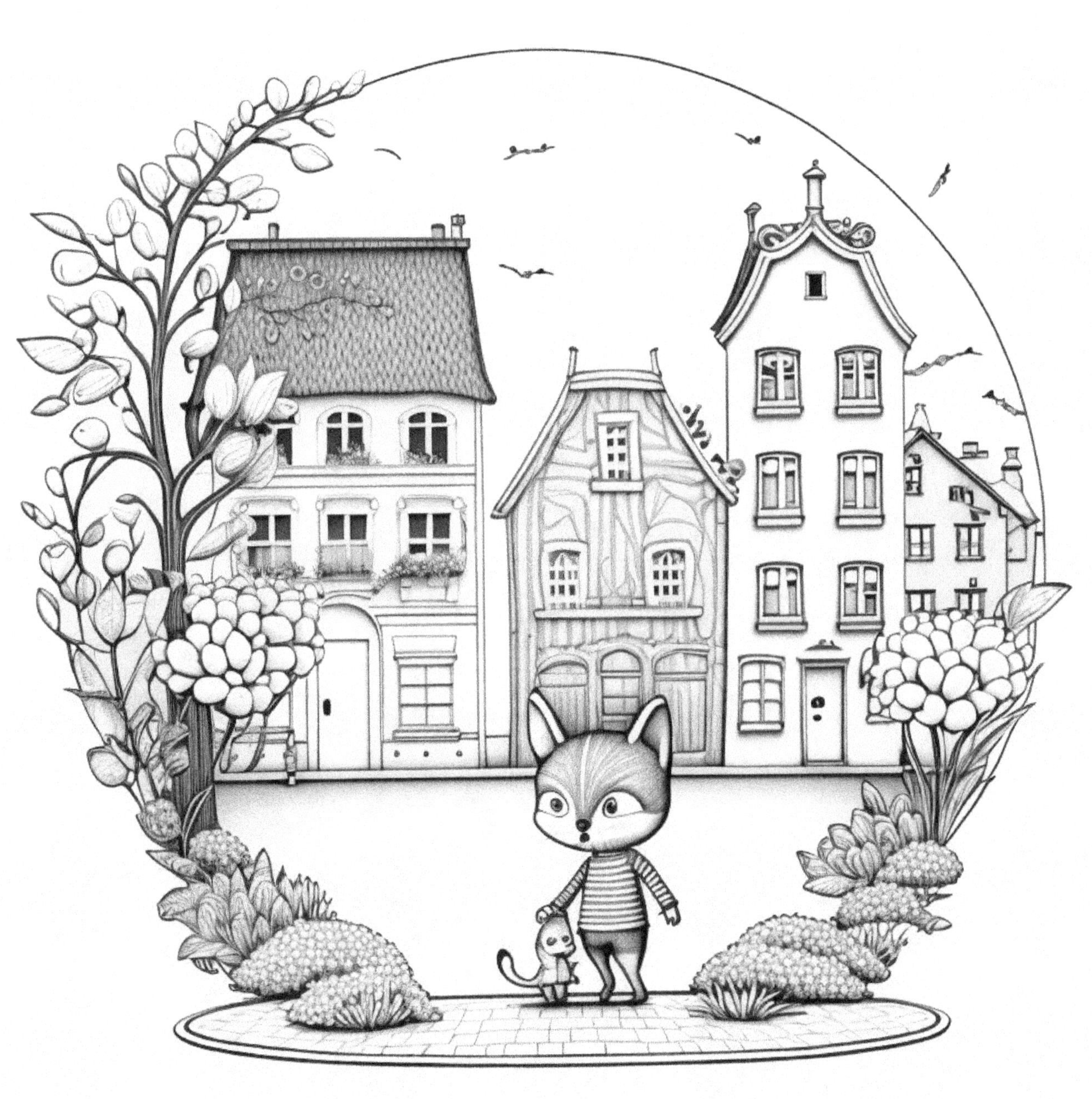

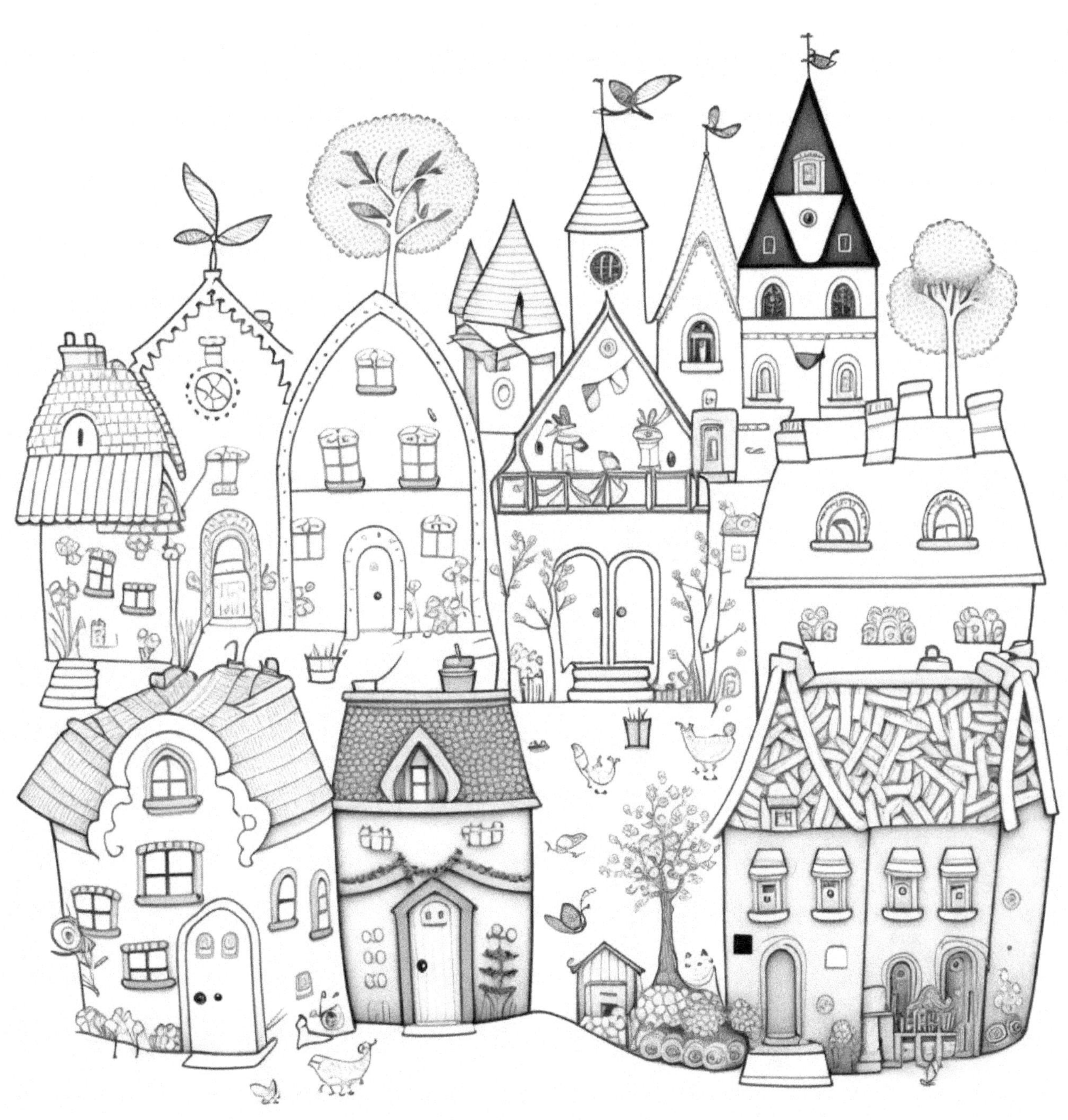

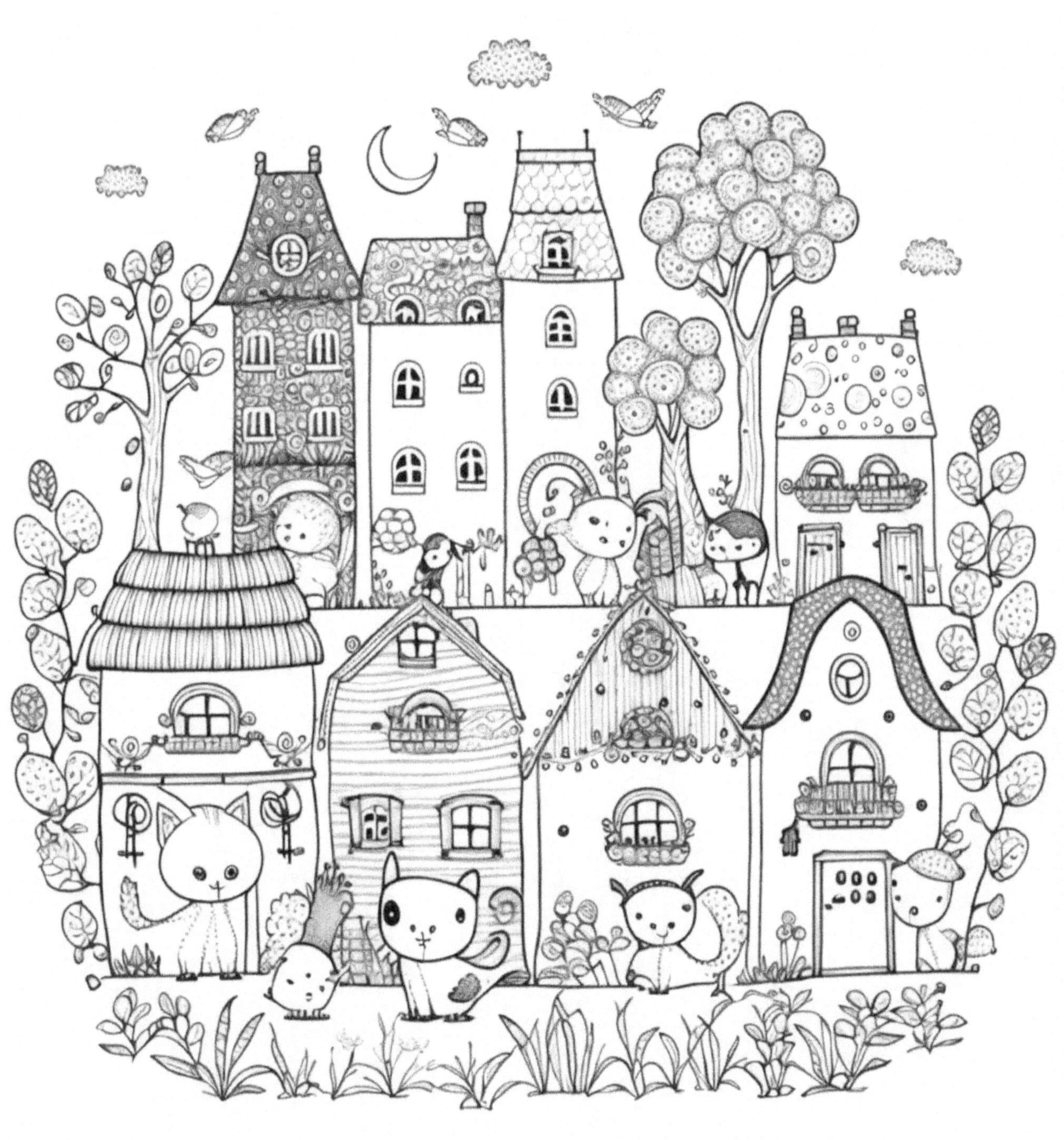

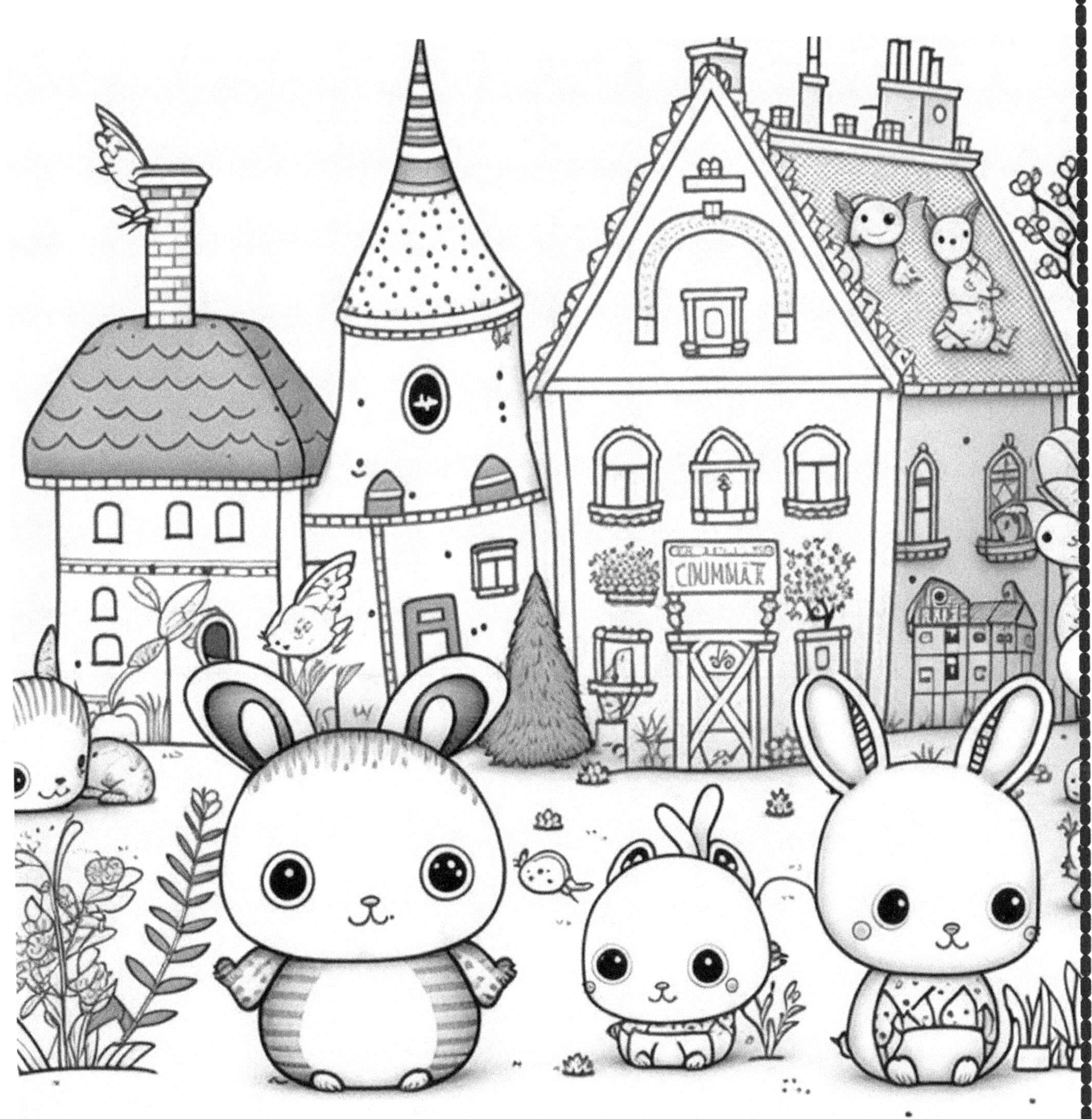

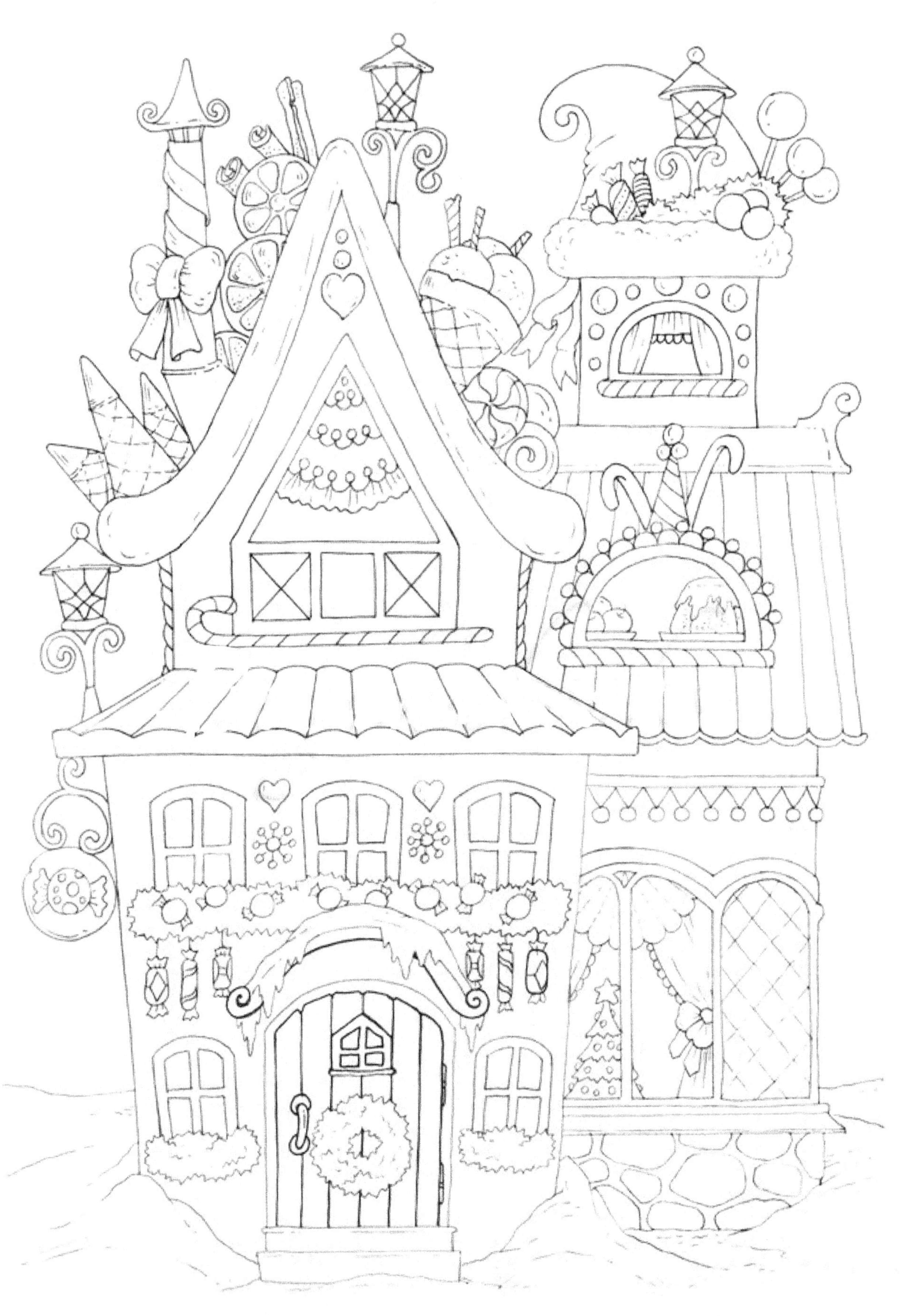

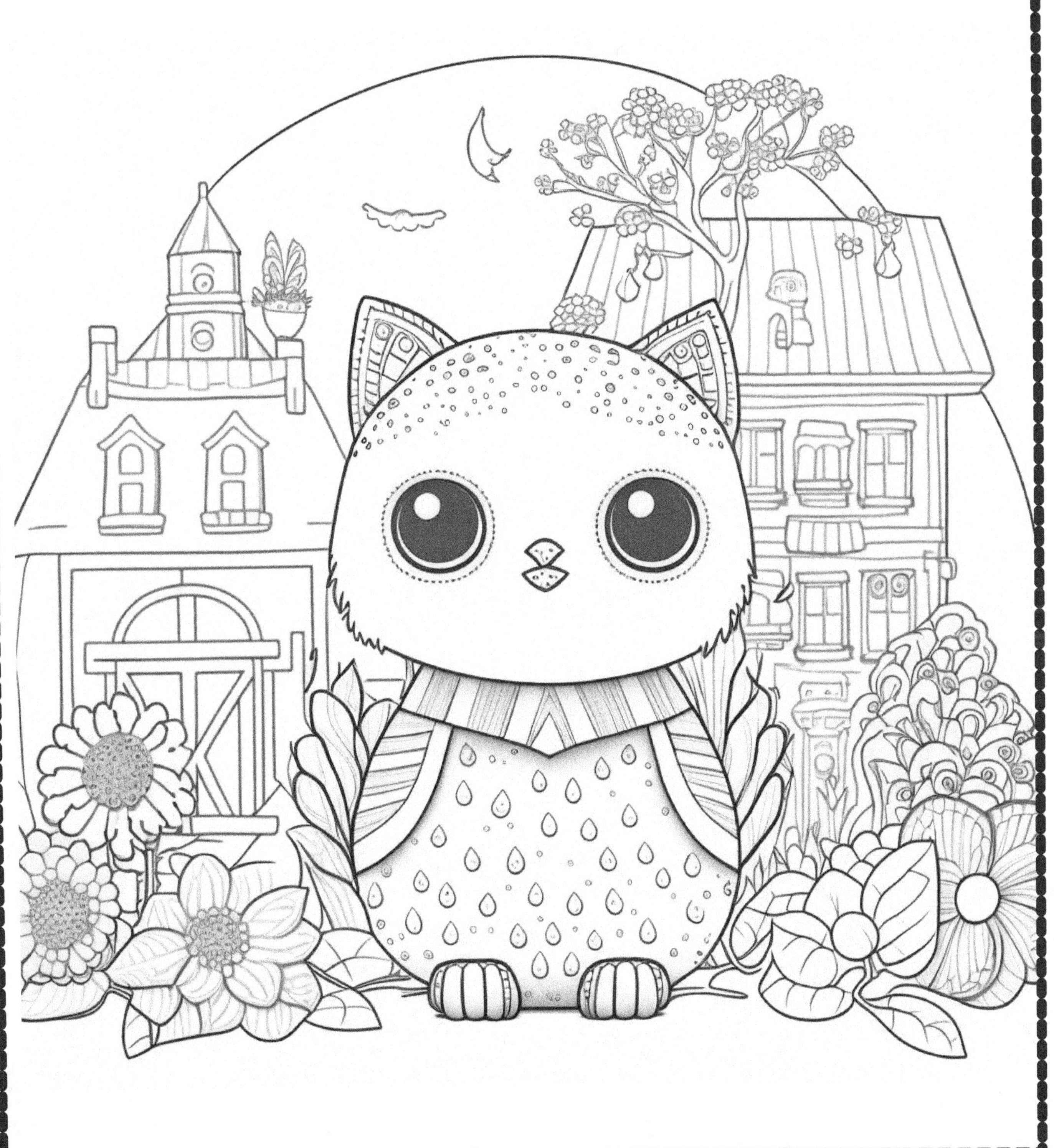

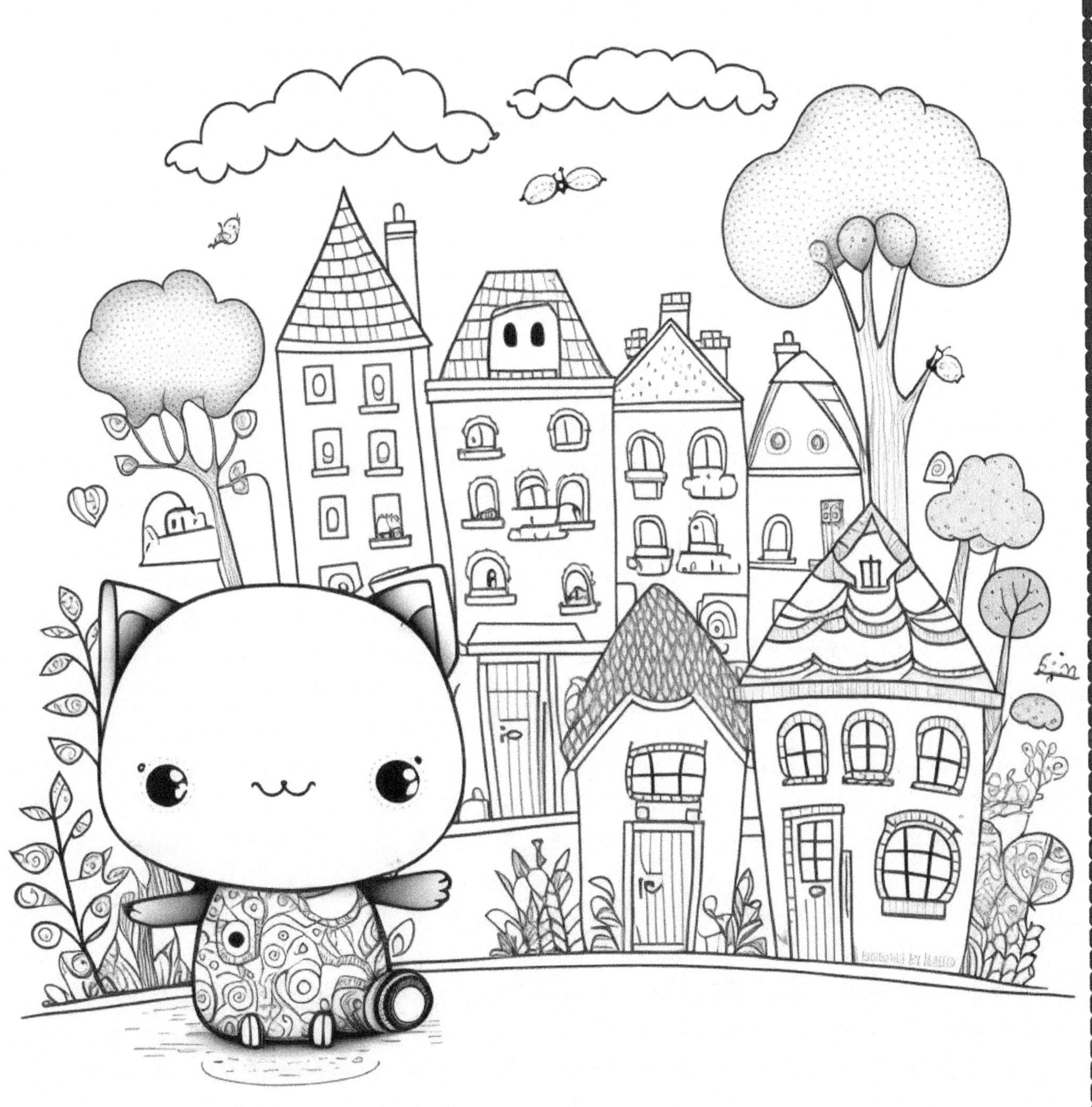

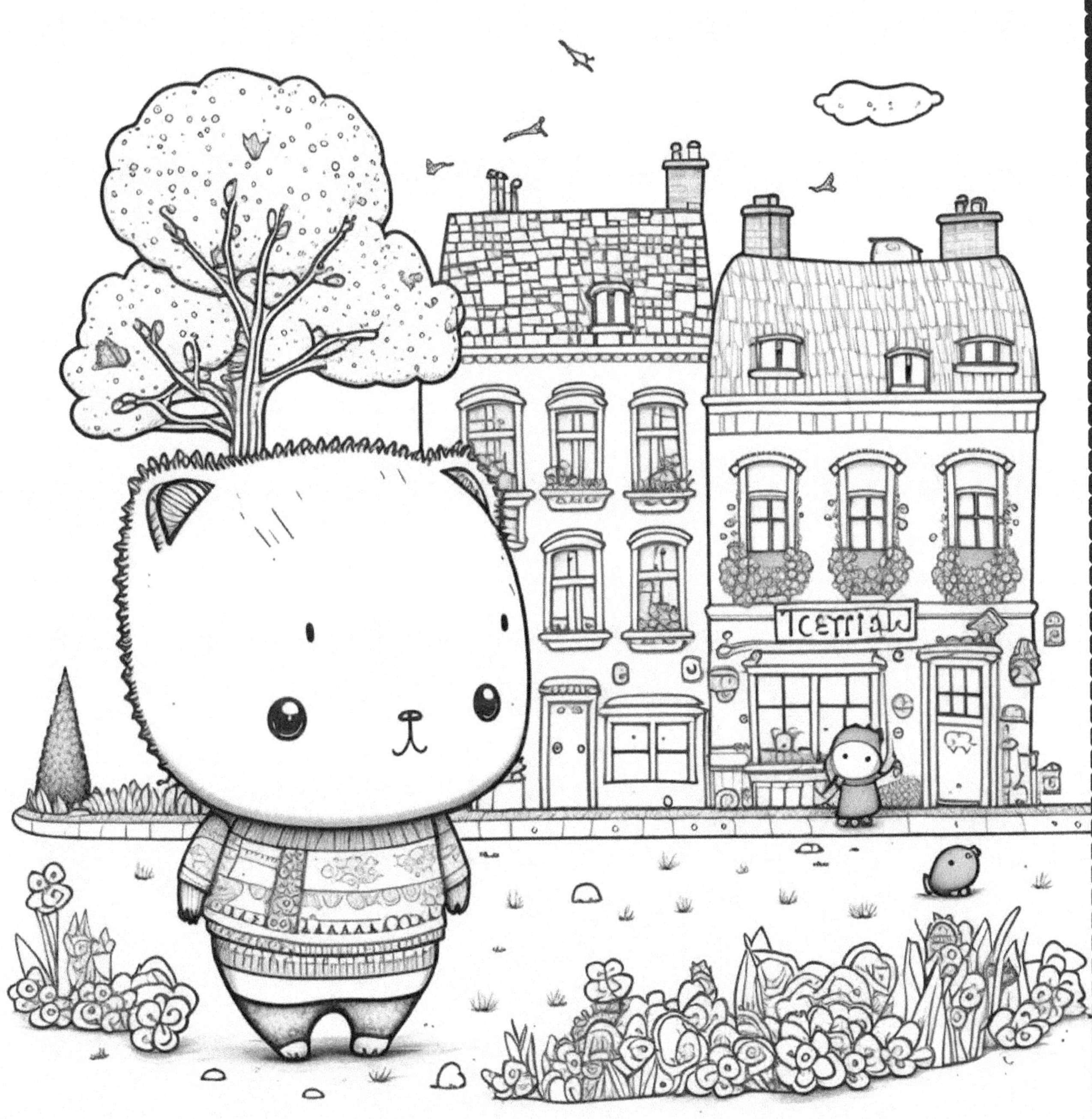

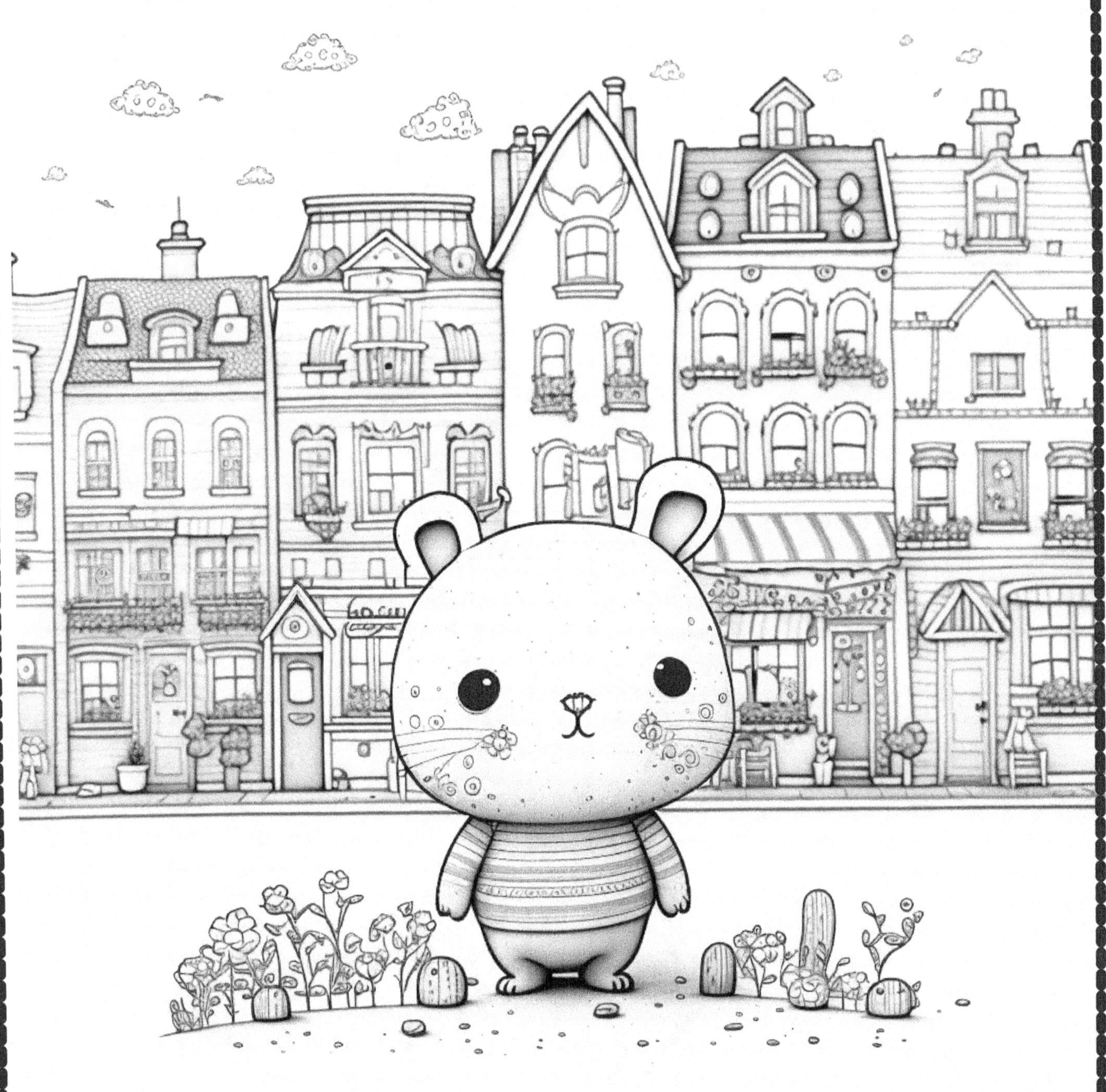

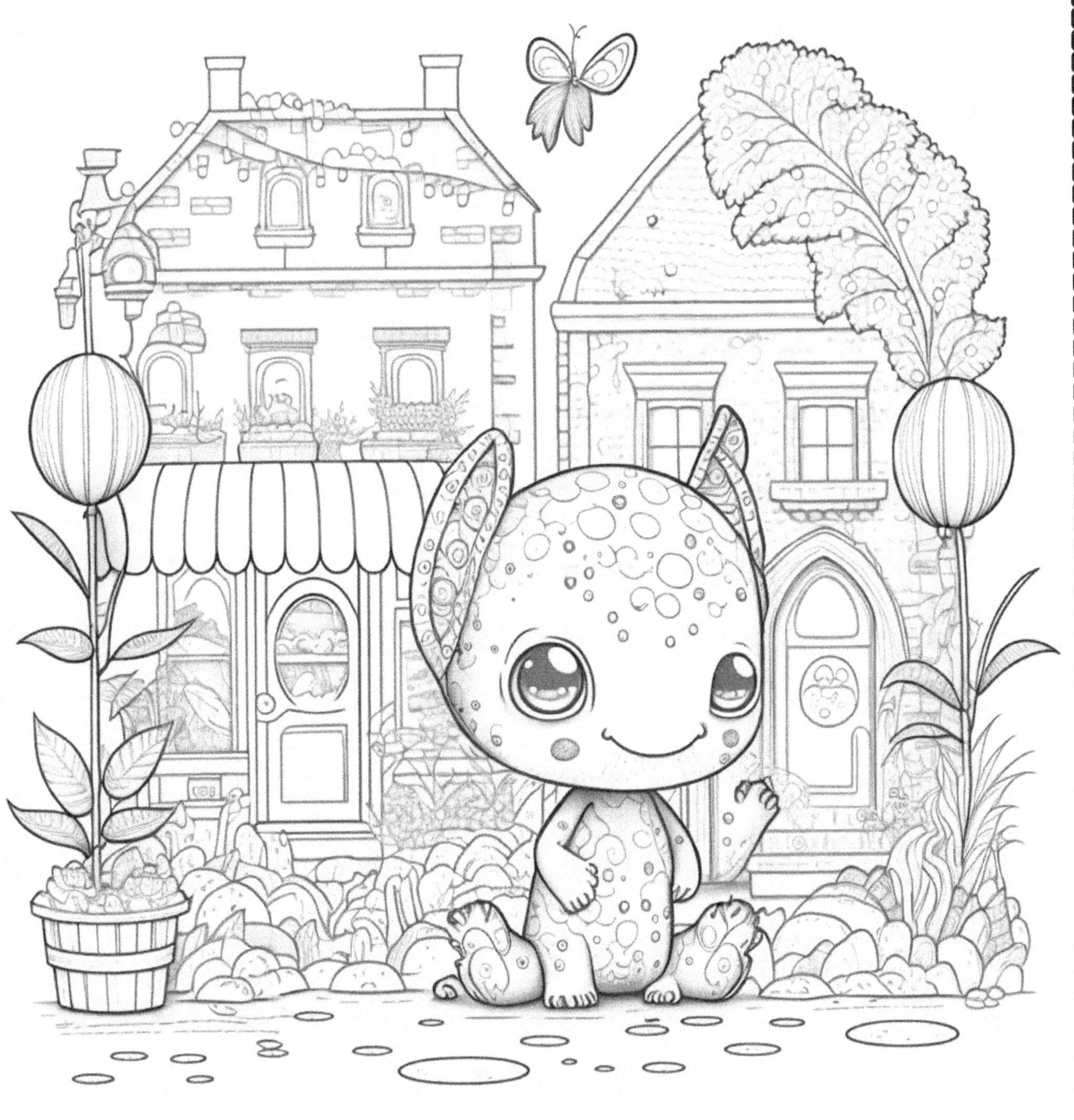

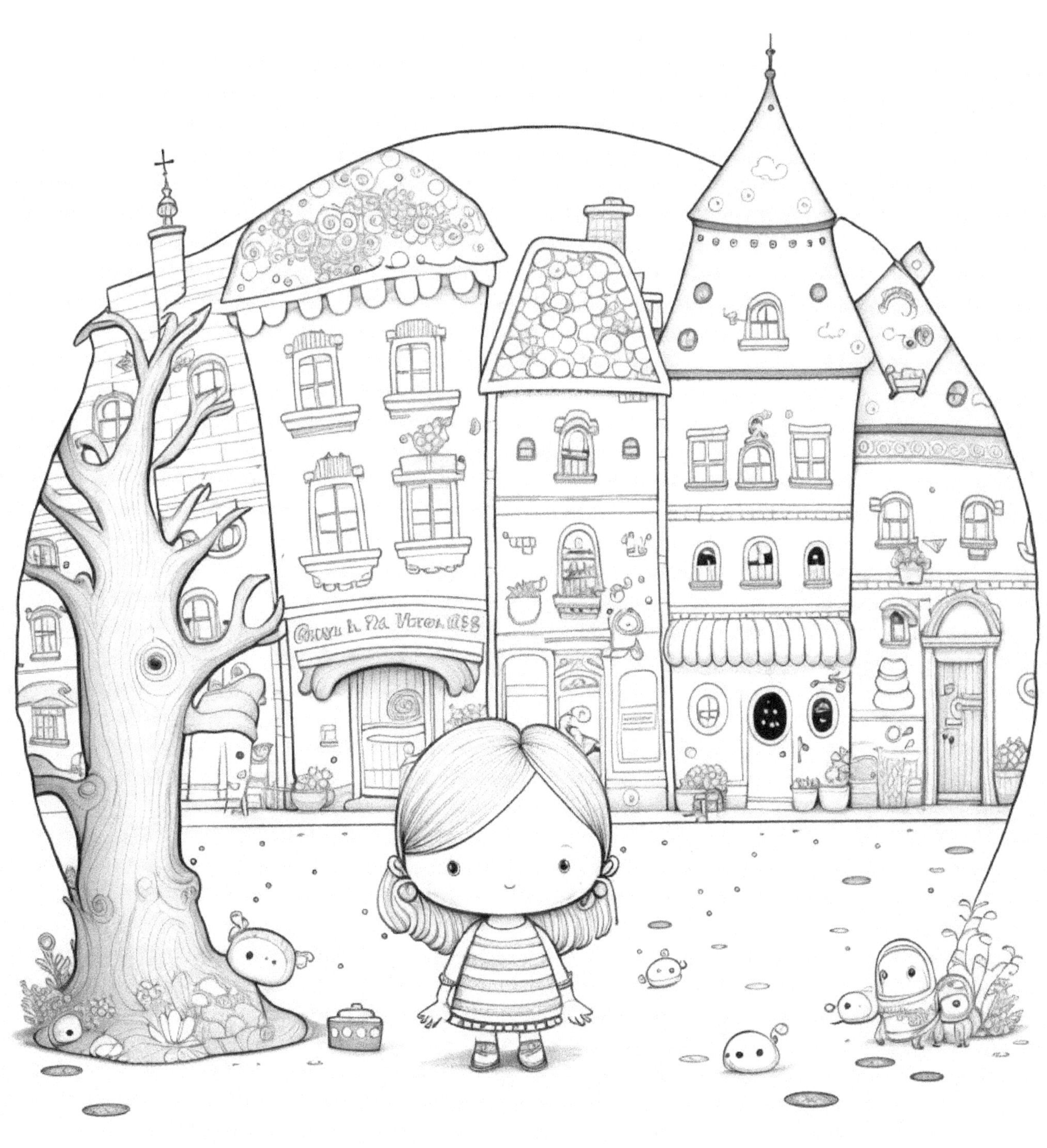

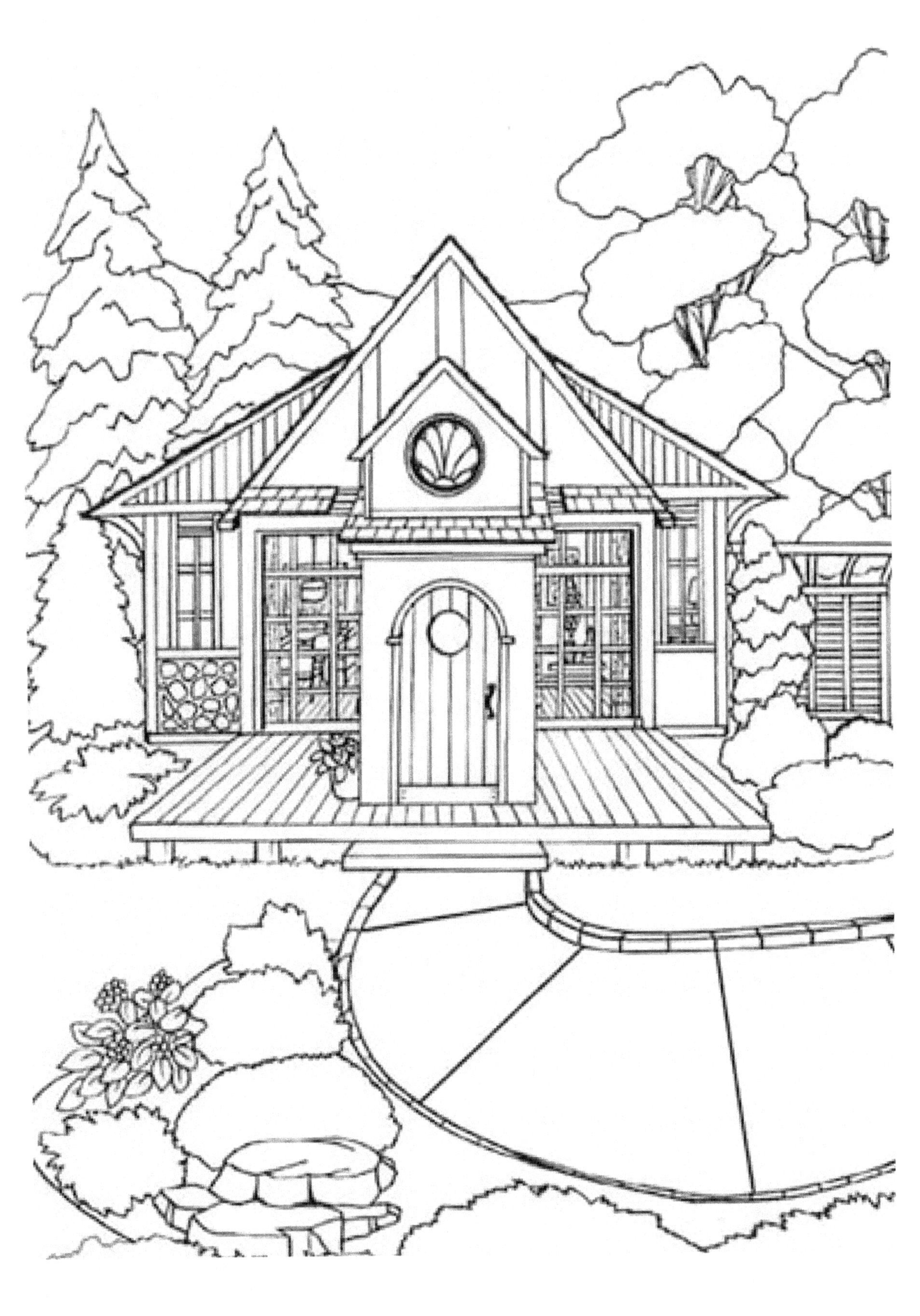

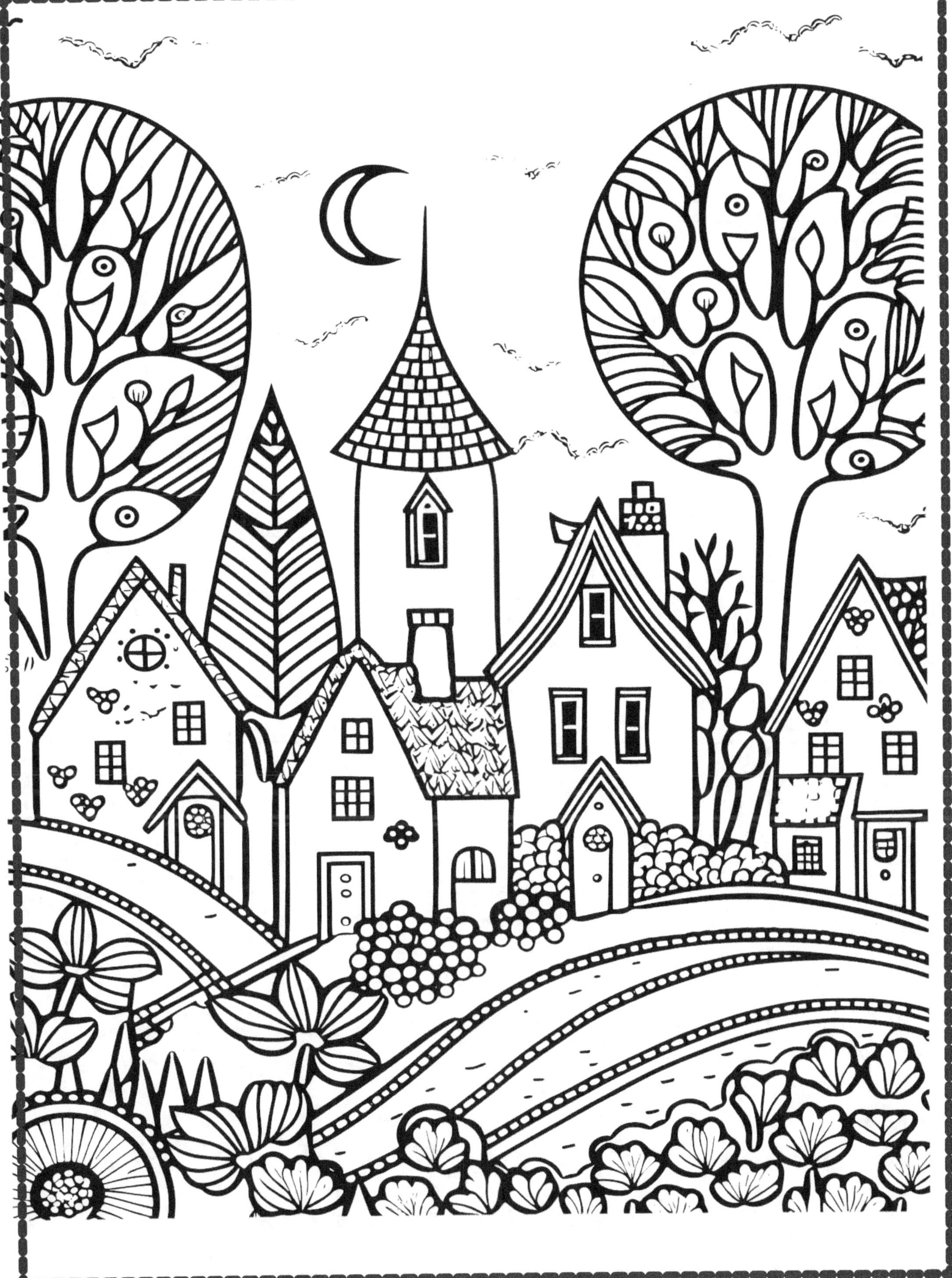

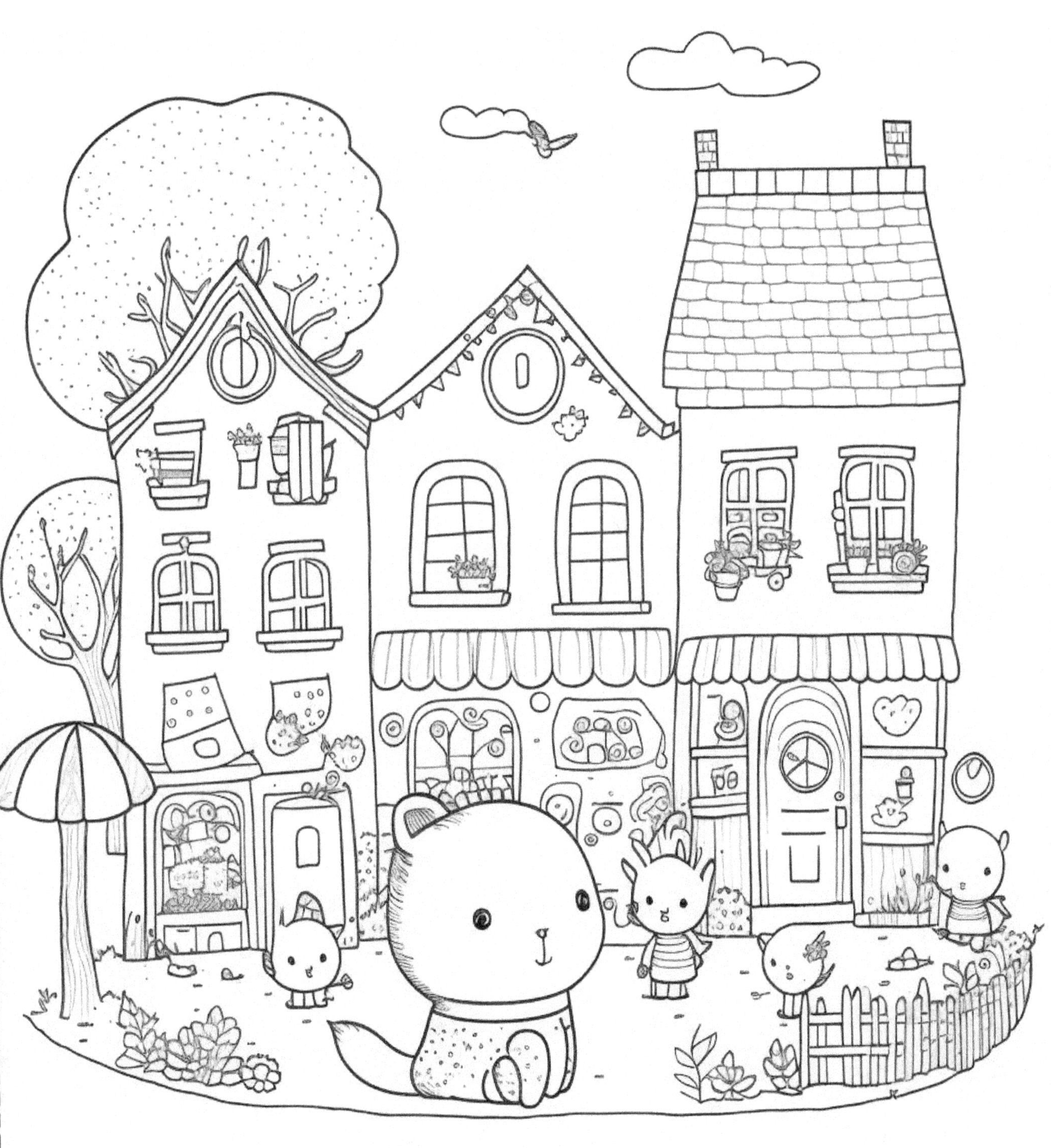

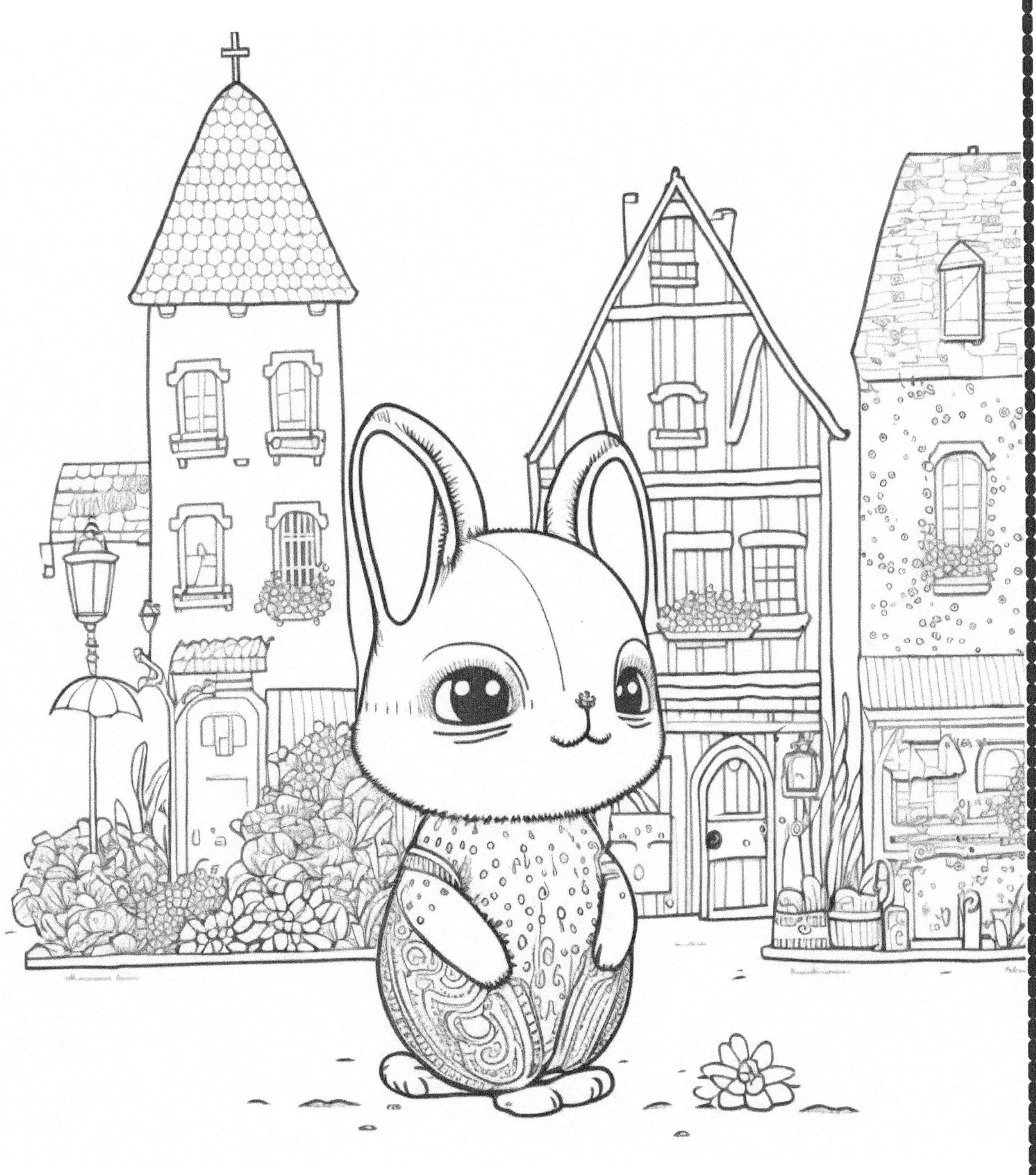

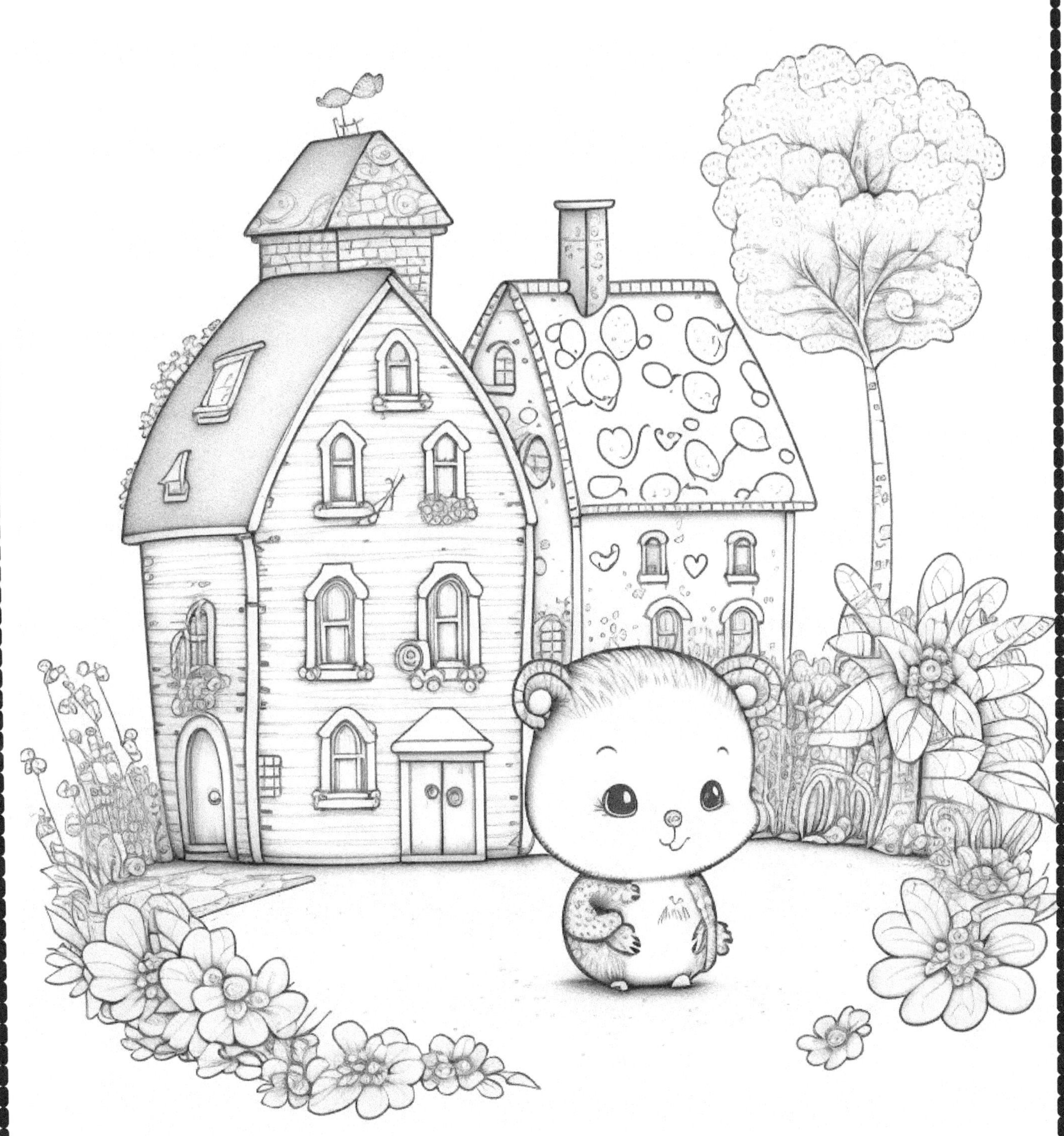

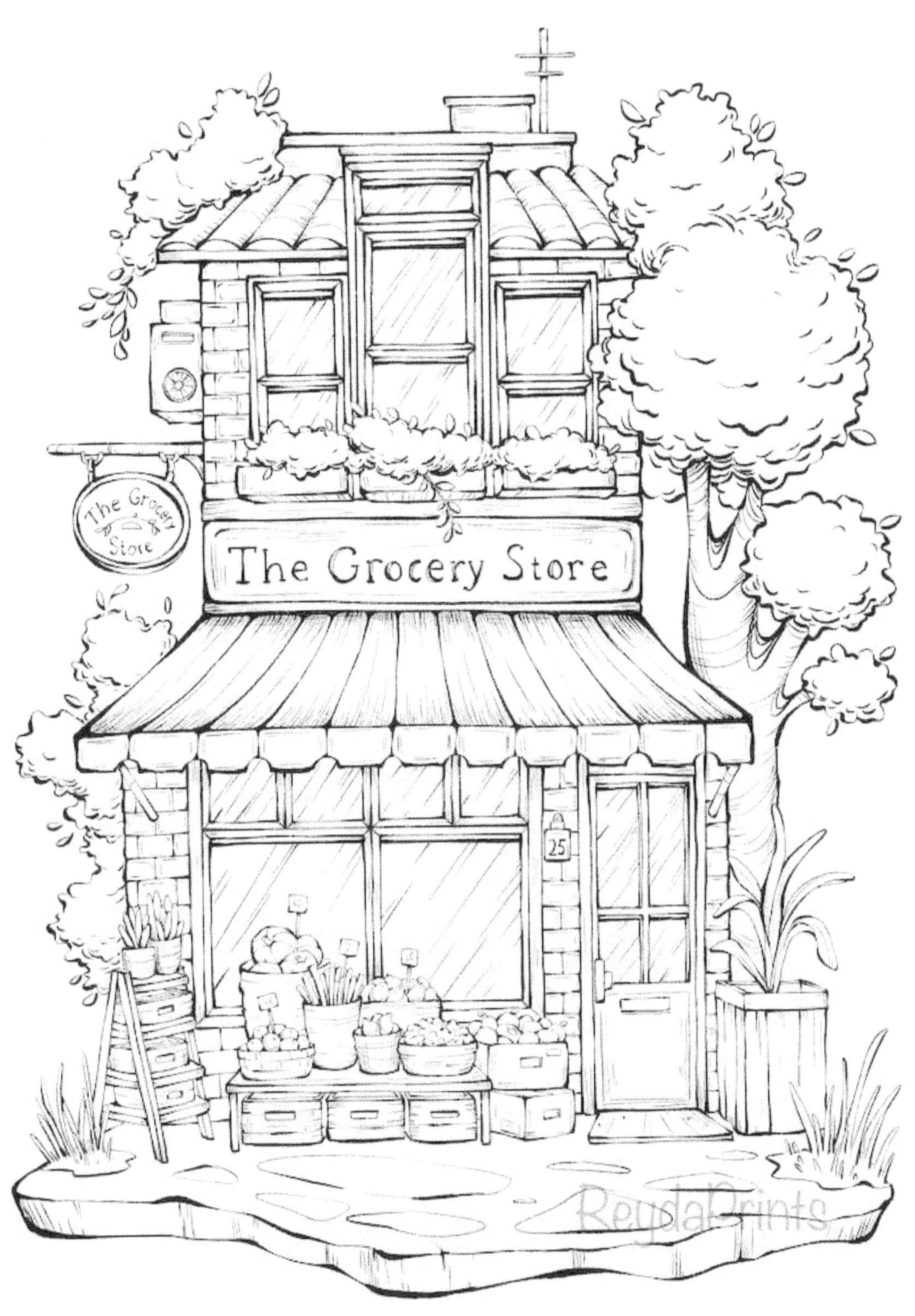

The Grocery Store
The Grocery Store
25

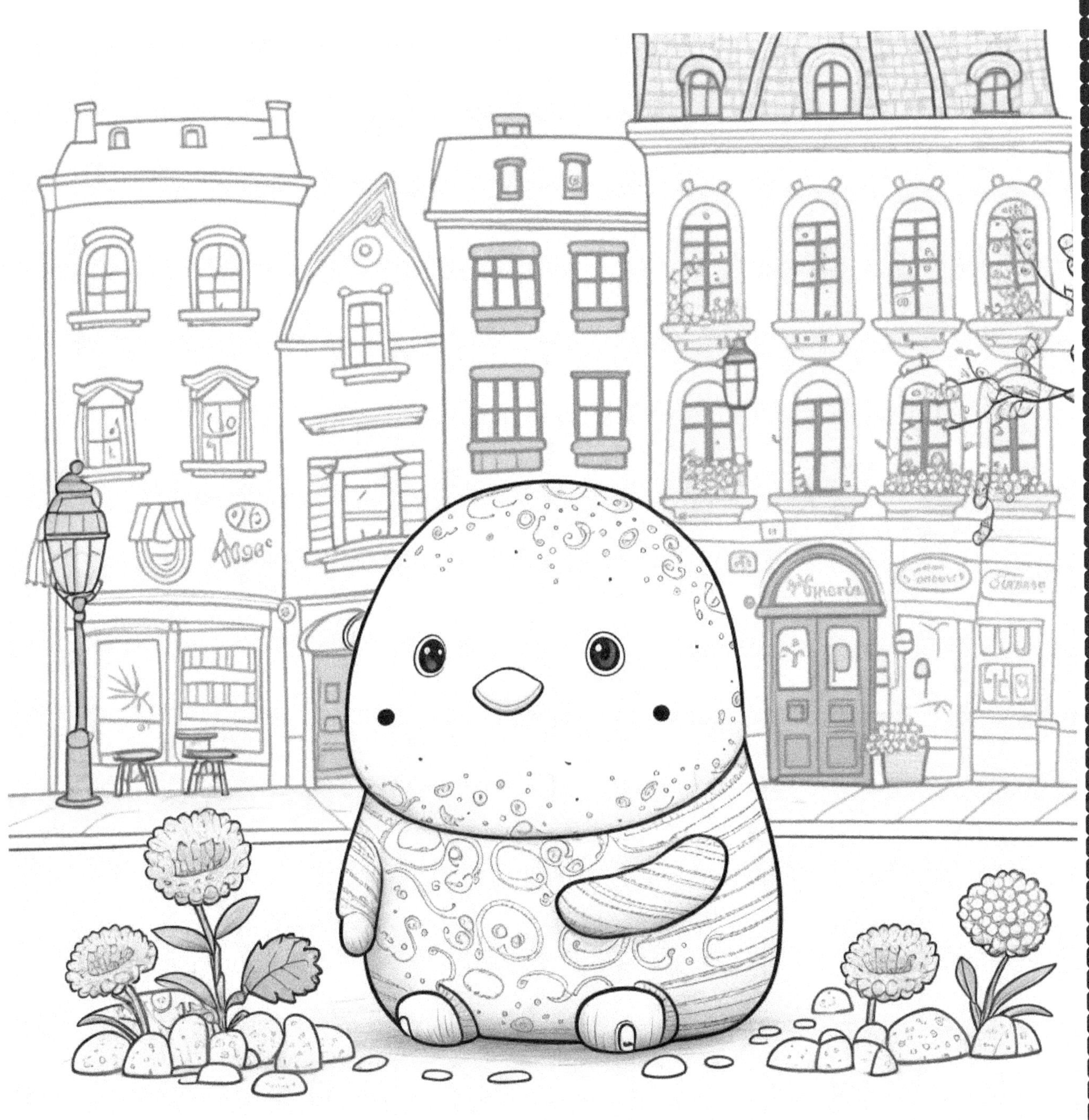

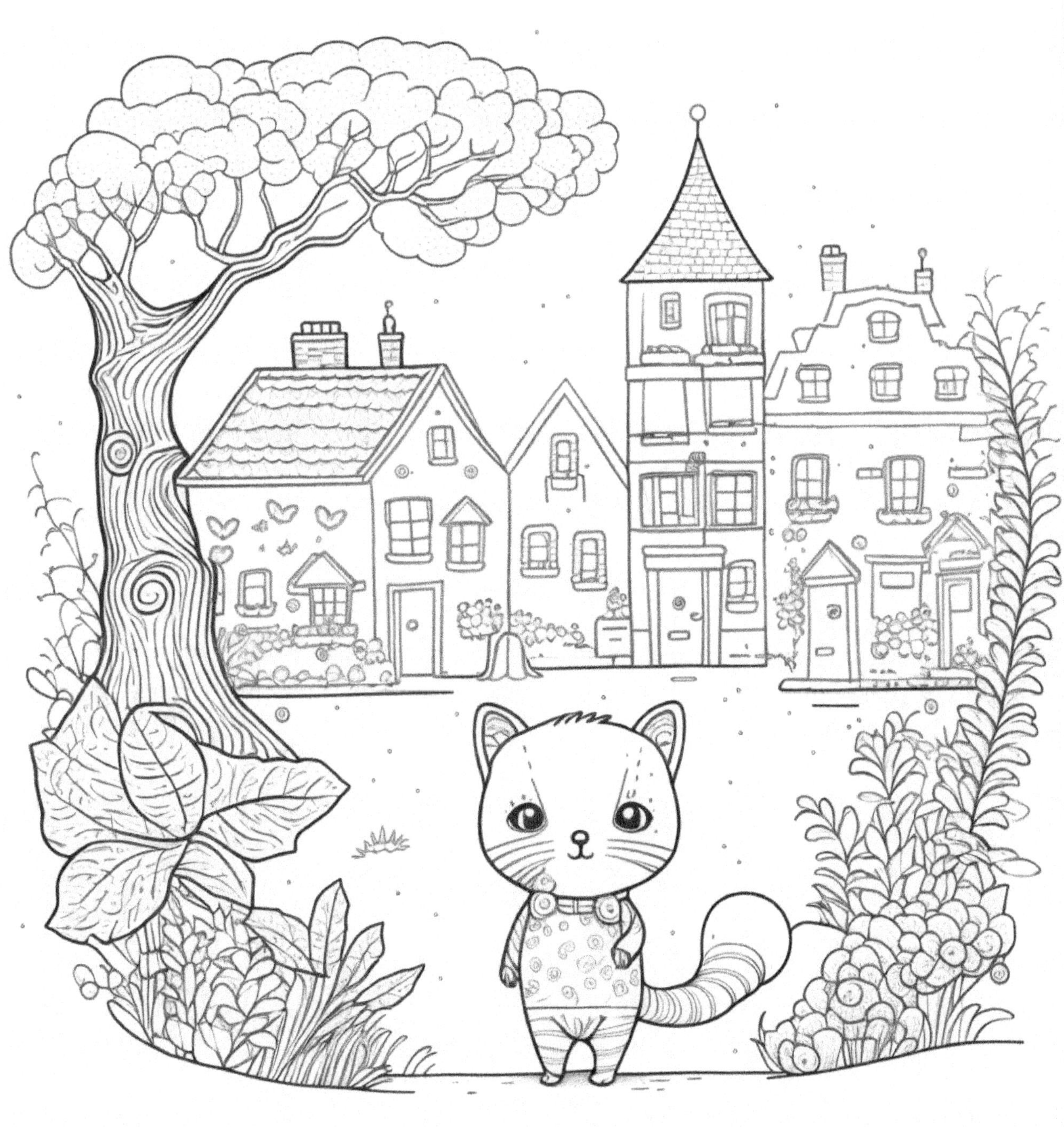

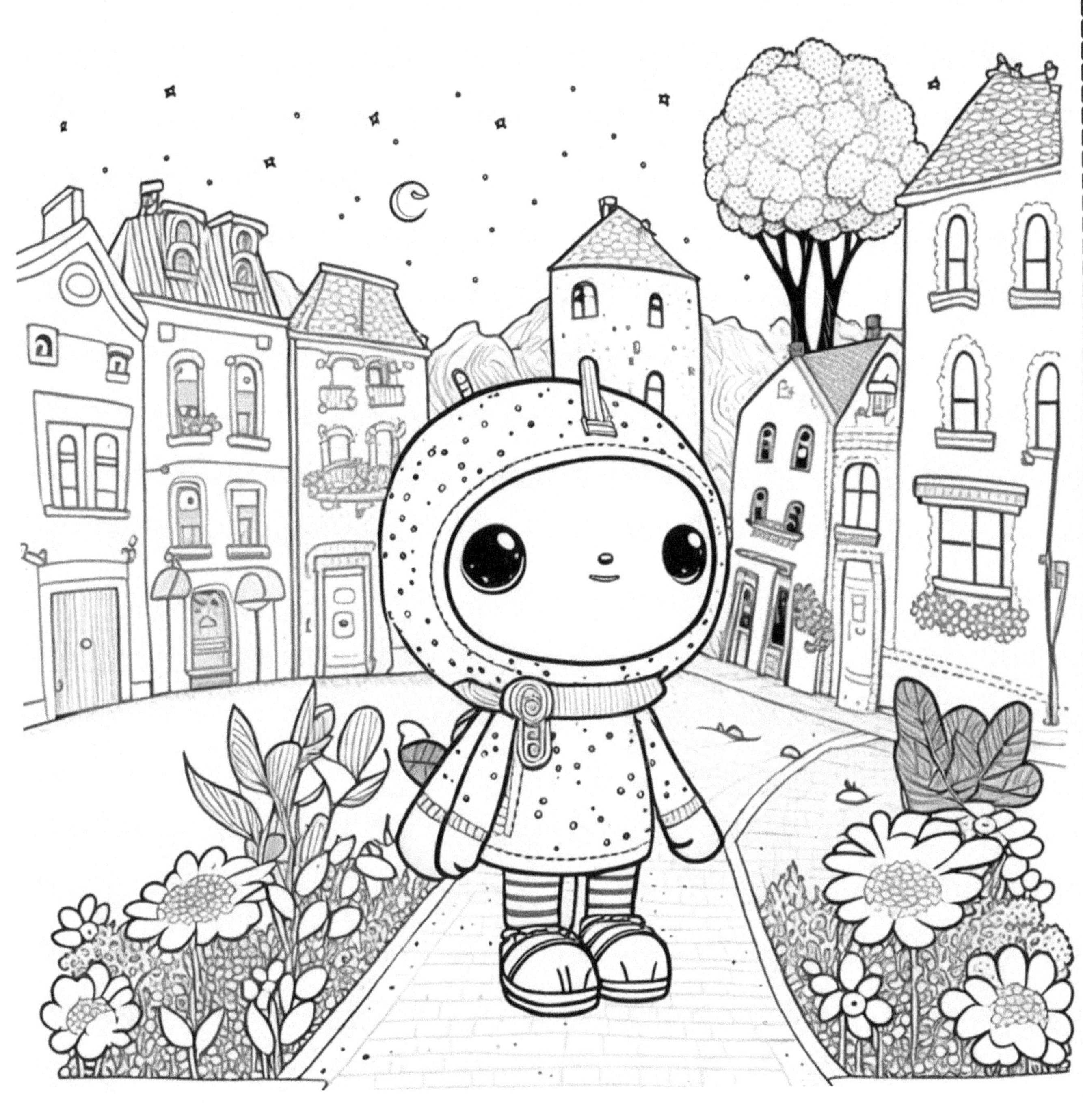

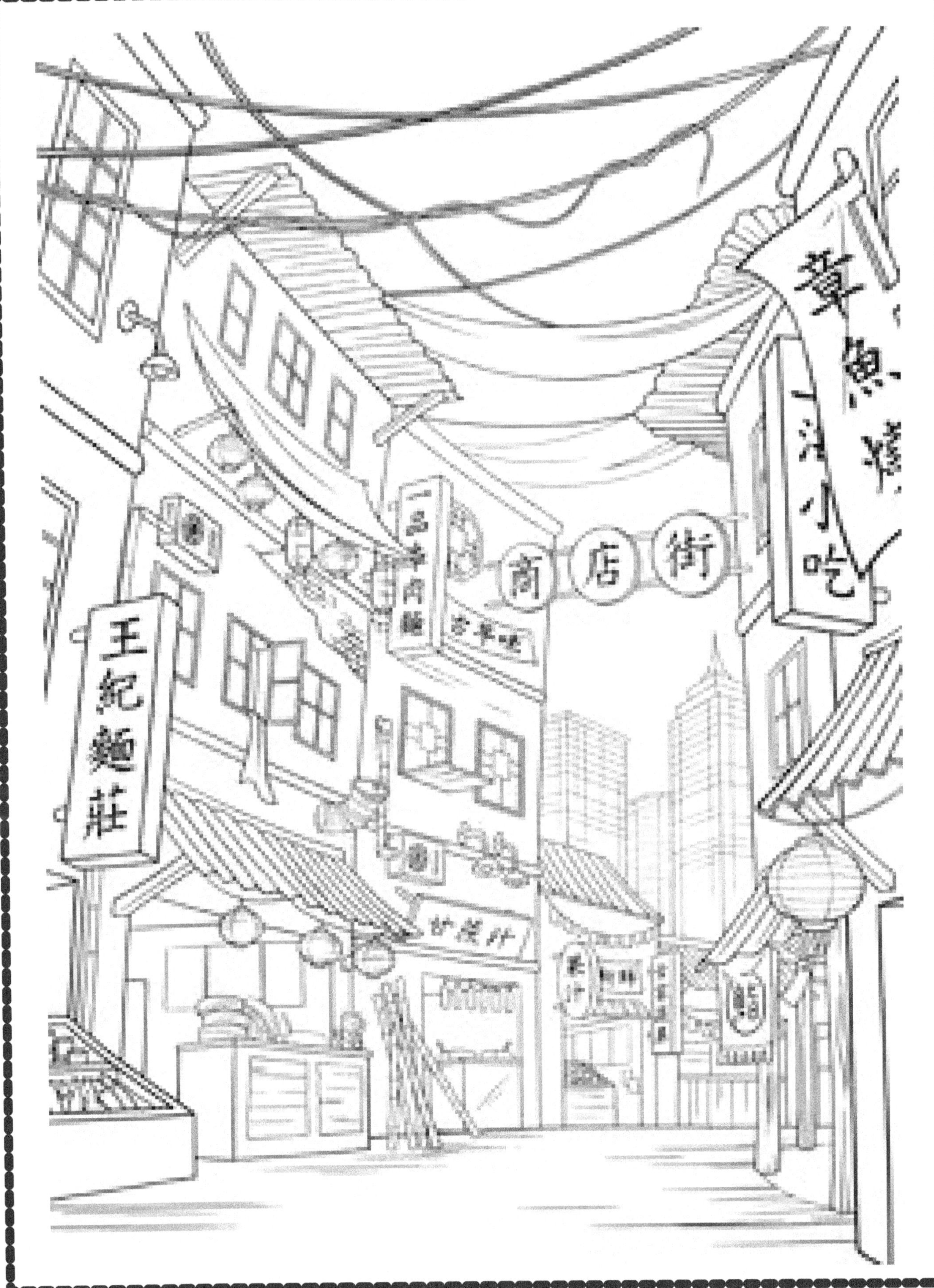
章魚燒
上洋小吃
商店街
王紀麵莊

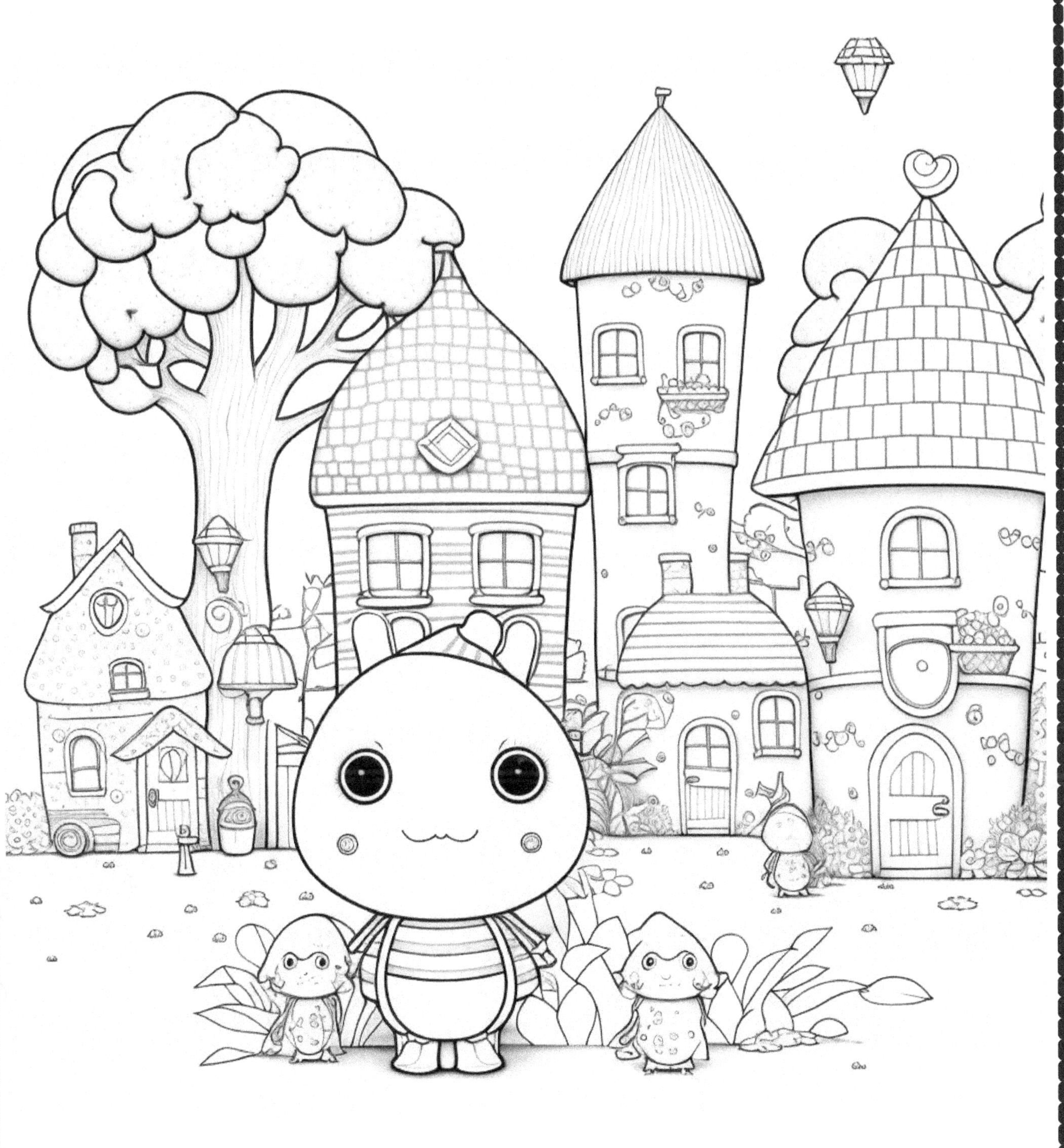

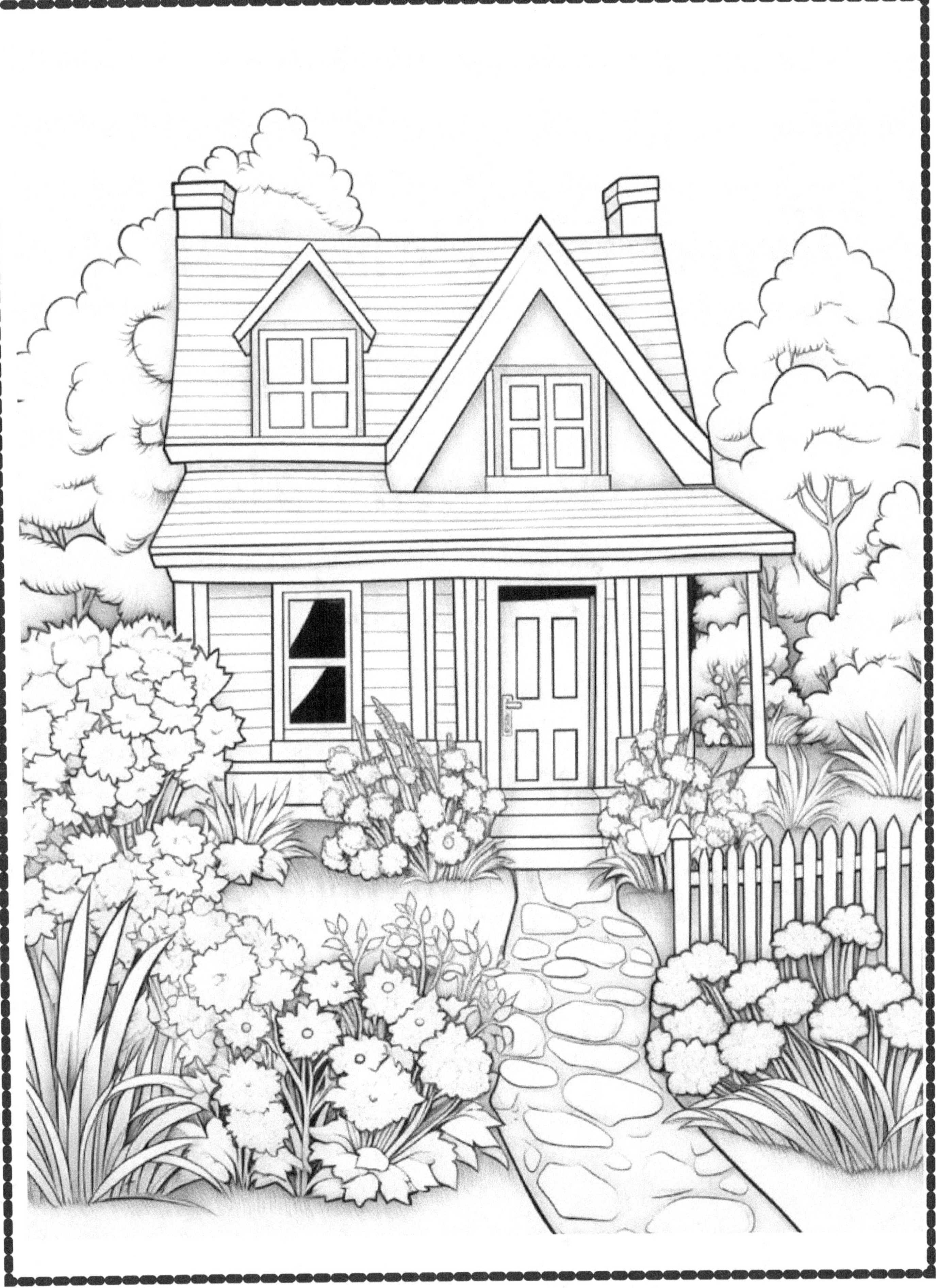

Thanks For Being With Us
I Hope We Are
Improved Your Adult
Education

So Don't Forget To
Check Your Others
Products On Our Author